The

GREAT

CHILES RELLENOS

BOOK

The
GREAT
CHILES RELLENOS
BOOK

Janos Wilder

Photographs by Laurie Smith

TEN SPEED PRESS
Berkeley | Toronto

10

Ten Speed Press
PO Box 7123
Berkeley, California 94707
www.tenspeed.com

Distributed in Australia by Simon and Schuster Australia,
in Canada by Ten Speed Press Canada, in New Zealand by
Southern Publishers Group, in South Africa by Real Books, and
in the United Kingdom and Europe by Publishers Group UK.

Cover and text design by Ed Anderson
Photography by Laurie Smith
Food styling by Erica McNeish

The photographs on pages 10 and 29 appear courtesy of
Rebecca Wilder.

The recipes for Chiles Rellenos de Carne on page 44, Chile
Verdes Rellenos on page 65, and Cadillo de Tomate on page
128 are adapted from *The Food and Life of Oaxaca: Traditional
Recipes from Mexico's Heart* by Zarela Martinez with permission
of John Wiley & Sons, Inc.

The recipe for Chiles en Nogado on pages 71–73 is adapted
from *The Cuisines of Mexico* by Diana Kennedy with permission.

Library of Congress Cataloging-in-Publication Data
Wilder, Janos.
  The great chiles rellenos book / Janos Wilder ;
photography by Laurie Smith.
      p. cm.
  Includes index.
  ISBN-13: 978-1-58008-854-1 (alk. paper)
  ISBN-10: 1-58008-854-6 (alk. paper)
  1. Cookery (Hot peppers). 2. Stuffed foods
(Cookery). 3. Cookery,
Mexican. I. Title.
  TX803.P46W55 2008
  641.6'384—dc22
                              2007041441

First printing, 2008
Printed in China

1 2 3 4 5 6 7 8 9 10 — 13 12 11 10 09 08

This book is for Rebecca, who encourages and nurtures my dreams with the patience and love that allows me to bring them to life.

Acknowledgments

This book came about thanks to Phil Wood, not only because he published it, but because his remarkable memory of the foods he loves includes the first rellenos I made for him in 1987. When it came time for this book, he thought of that Lobster and Brie Relleno and asked me to write it.

On a project like this, there are plenty of co-conspirators. Much appreciation goes out to mine, including my friends in Tucson and in Gold Hill, Colorado, who probably ate far more rellenos than they wanted during the recipe testing, and especially to Rebecca, who told me she put on 7 pounds while I was cooking for this book.

Veronica, thank you for bringing your enthusiasm, focus, and passion to this project that ended up in your lap at the last minute. Your guidance has helped shape the look and feel of what we've produced. Also many thanks to our photographer, Laurie Smith, who transformed my recipes into the stunning visual images you see here. Much gratitude is also due to our designer, Ed Anderson, who made everything fit beautifully into a challenging format.

My cooking takes place on a continuum of traditions created by great cooks whose purposes were the loftiest: feeding their families and communities. They cooked with love and from necessity and provided a firm base from which I have the luxury to take the culinary flights of fancy that have created this book.

Contents

UNTRADITIONAL, TRADITIONAL
CHEESE CHILES RELLENOS

continued

CHILES RELLENOS CASSEROLES, POPPERS, AND SALADS

SIDE DISHES AND SIDE SALADS

═ DRESSINGS, SALSAS, RELISHES, AND SAUCES ═

Why I Make the Rellenos I Make

I sampled my first relleno in 1978 on a courtship trip to Tucson with my wife-to-be, Rebecca. We had met several months earlier in the small mountain town of Gold Hill, Colorado, where she taught kindergarten through second grade in the two-room schoolhouse that served the community of 125 residents. I was chef at the Gold Hill Inn, and Rebecca was waiting tables there over the summer. At the end of the season, she returned to Tucson to be near her family and to reenroll at the University of Arizona with the goal of starting a second career in graphic design. I followed—with the goal of making Rebecca my wife.

Tucson at that time was the self-declared, unofficial Mexican-food capital of the world. So off we went to one of the city's many Mexican restaurants. Rebecca ordered a red chile and bean burrito, one of her favorite dishes to this day. I ordered a chile relleno. It was, well, disappointing. The batter was doughy, thick, and heavy, while the chile itself was thin, torn, and tasteless, and the cheese was processed—need I say more?

The good news is that Rebecca returned with me to Gold Hill where she continued to teach and I continued to cook for a couple of more years. This was followed by a stint in Santa Fe and a wonderful experience cooking in the Bordeaux region of France. In 1983 we were back in Tucson opening our first restaurant, Janos, on the grounds of the Tucson Museum of Art.

Around this time, I was determined to learn about and understand traditional Mexican ingredients and cooking techniques. It was my hope to then apply these insights to the sensibilities I had gained from French culinary philosophy and my experiences working in France.

In order to learn more about the cooking of a region, it's important to identify its more significant, iconic dishes—dishes that help tell the story of a region's culinary heritage, or "cultural culinary icons" as I call them. I consider dishes like enchiladas, seviches, chiles rellenos, and tacos in this category because each of them tells me something special about Mexican culture, about how and what people eat, and about how ingredients are used. To fully understand each dish, I desconstruct it into an "ideal type." In other words, I want to start with the purest form.

Chiles rellenos, like most Mexican foods, are "of the people." Recipes are handed down from generation to generation, and like all great dishes, *everyone* has an opinion about them—the best ways to make them, whose mother makes them best, or where to get the best one. For relleno purists, some of the recipes in this book may constitute heresy; however, for the more adventurous cook, the recipes will open up new worlds of possibilities.

The word *relleno* means "stuffed," so I started with a stuffed chile. In order to stuff the chile, it first has be peeled and seeded, so I explored the different ways to peel and seed chiles. For a chile to hold its stuffing successfully, the flesh must be firm and intact. That led me to the roasting and peeling techniques I describe here.

If the chile is too spicy, it will overwhelm the flavors in the stuffing and you won't taste them. So I needed to find chiles that had the proper levels of heat. I also needed to obtain chiles that were appropriately sized to hold a sufficient amount of stuffing. In Tucson, the rellenos at that time were filled with cheese, but in Mexico we discovered a variety of meat fillings as well. It would be a while before I found vegetable, fish, and fruit rellenos, but just thinking about the possibilities kept me searching.

Breaking away from the dairy limitations allowed me to explore a whole new world of ingredients and flavors that might or might not be found in more traditional Mexican cooking. In the end, it wasn't enough for me to know how to make a great *typical* chile relleno—I wanted to know how to make a great relleno, period.

Similarly, I began to experiment with different batters and crusts, sauces, salsas, relishes, and salads that would complement the chiles and fillings I was making. Some were traditional, many were not. This experimentation led to the creation of many of the recipes on my restaurant menus, and I've added to my repertoire over the years. Many of my favorites are included here.

I've made thousands of rellenos, and while they're usually eaten at lunch or dinner, I included a breakfast relleno recipe that incorporates many of my favorite Mexican breakfast foods. Rellenos are traditionally served with side dishes such as beans, guacamole, and salsa. In most restaurants, they are served as combination plates or as entrees.

Sometimes rellenos are part of a celebration, like the wonderful Chiles en Nogado rediscovered in Laura Esquivel's provocative and magical novel, *Like Water for Chocolate*. Originally created in Puebla to celebrate Mexico's independence from Spain, Chiles en Nogado has become celebrated among the country's many legendary dishes. Rellenos are also served for Día de los Muertos (Day of the Dead) in November, and indeed find themselves on many Mexican menus at holiday meals throughout the year.

The relleno recipes included here range from traditional to unconventional to downright exotic. My approach to the relleno is the same as my approach to cooking in general: I learn how and why dishes were developed in the past, use those traditions as points of exploration and departure, and combine ingredients and techniques that work well together and, most important, taste great. (You may be surprised to discover that the "new" rellenos don't actually cover new ground. In fact, all the recipes use familiar ingredients and techniques.)

Making chiles rellenos is a blast and a great communal effort. So invite some friends over, make some limonada or a pitcher of margaritas, or crack open an icy beer, and let everyone get in on the action—from roasting the chiles to deciding what you're going to stuff into them, from soaking the beans to making them into silky refritos—enjoy the process, and savor the results. Most important, have fun!

ABOUT
CHILES

ABOUT CHILES

Basic Flavors

In its simplest form, Mexican cooking weaves three flavor profiles through its dishes. Often piquant flavors are moderated by deep flavors, with proteins intertwining their flavors between the two. Think of a basic dish that has found its way into the Americanization of Mexican food: the simple combination plate of beans and/or rice, an enchilada, and salsa. In this example, the salsa is the high note that opens your palate and titillates your senses. The beans or rice are typically not made to be spicy hot but are used to put out any fire caused by the salsa. The enchilada contains the primary flavors of the dish and will have flavor profiles that, in terms of heat, will range between the salsa and the rice and beans. While this is a simplistic example, the pattern holds throughout the cooking of the region. Whether in fish dishes from Veracruz, Oaxacan barbacoa, the parillas in Sonora, or the *alto cocina* in Mexico City, you will find similar flavor combinations everywhere.

When I first started working with the flavors, ingredients, and dishes of Mexico, I used this basic pattern as my guide. In fact, when venturing into *any* uncharted culinary territory, I always use this flavor pattern as a touchstone. The reason it works is that it not only satisfies, but it also keeps the food interesting and alive. Thomas Keller, one of the country's foremost chefs and culinary visionaries, talks about the appropriateness of the meal that is made of a number of small courses. He argues that too much of any one dish gets boring. He has a valid point, and Mexican cooking is inherently geared to keeping things interesting. If your palate gets heavy with the starch, a bite of salsa will perk things up. If the salsa is a bit too hot, the beans will cool things off. And the flavors in between keep things exciting.

The relleno dishes presented here incorporate the same pattern but expand on the world of possibilities it creates. Having spent time cooking in France, and because I've always been enamored by French culinary sensibilities, the first relleno I created back in 1987 was Lobster and Brie Rellenos with Nantua Sauce. To make it, an Anaheim chile was quickly roasted, peeled, and seeded. For the filling, I sautéed fresh lobster meat in Pernod (the French anise-flavored liquor), a tiny bit of chipotle in adobo (smoked jalapeño in vinegar, tomato, and garlic), and a little butter, then blended the lobster meat with soft, rich, triple crème Brie. This was stuffed into the chile, which I dipped into a very light beer batter and cooked until the batter was crisp and the cheese started to melt and run. For the base flavor, I made a sauce from the lobster shells and some crayfish I had around (yes, I know, it's pretty great to have the larder of a professional kitchen at your disposal). Instead of a salsa, I made a small salad of jicama (the crunchy tuber found in Mexico and Central America), lime, and Cilantro Aioli. I put it on the menu and had an instant hit on my hands. Although the ingredients are different than the beans, enchiladas, and salsa combo described earlier, the flavor pattern is exactly the same. The rich, mild, and flavorful nantua sauce helps to ground this dish and, along with the refreshing jicama salad, puts out any fires caused by the chipotle or the Anaheim chile. The lobster and Brie are the luxurious, decadent flavors that carry the dish. Every bite is interesting and exciting.

A (Very) Brief History

The chile pepper is an ancient native species of the New World. In Peru, there is archeological evidence of chile peppers at burial sites dating back more than 8,000 years. The Mayans cultivated many types of chiles, and the Aztec and pre-Columbian civilizations used chiles extensively in their diets. Some wild chiles, including the chiltepíns, grew as far north as the Sonoran Desert (and still do), but it was Spanish settlers who were responsible for spreading and cultivating other varieties of chiles in Arizona and New Mexico, beginning in the late 1500s. Before that time there is little evidence to suggest that chiles were being used by North American Indians in this region.

With the Spanish, chile cultivation proliferated, and chiles were soon found all over what is today the American Southwest. Among the chiles that adapted well to the region was the long green chile from New Mexico (consequently called the New Mexico chile), which came to be known as the Anaheim chile when it was taken to California in the early 1900s. In fact, once in California the New Mexico chile not only got a name change but was also bred to be milder. So now they are two distinctly different chiles.

As the cultivation of chiles expanded over time, several distinct varieties developed as the chile adapted to different environments. All chiles are in the family of Nightshade (Solanaceae) and in the same genus of Capscum. All the chiles in this book are in the same species: annum. Within the species there are hundreds of cultivars (horticultural varieties), and the varieties are known by many different common names.

Recently, agriculturalists have focused on the chile in an effort to try to control its heat, size, growth, and resistance to predators. This hybridization causes considerable confusion in the naming of chiles. For instance, what I call the Anaheim, is, as noted above, actually a milder descendent of the New Mexico green chile. Ed Curry, who owns Curry Seed & Chile Company in Pearce, Arizona, about forty miles south of Tucson, has been hybridizing varieties of green chiles and selectively breeding them to create a strain that has uniform heat, grows reliably, and whose fruit begins to grow about one foot above the ground, making it easy to harvest with mechanical equipment. For the last several years, Ed has been selling his seeds to commercial growers all over the world. Today, chiles I buy from elsewhere, such as the legendary produce from Hatch, New Mexico, are actually grown from seeds produced right here in southern Arizona.

The Best Chiles for the Best Rellenos

When choosing the best chiles to use for rellenos, several factors should be considered. First, you don't want to work with a chile that will be too hot and mask the flavor of your filling. Neither do you want a chile with little flavor and no heat. The chile itself is more than just a vehicle for the stuffing. Its flavor is an integral part of the dish. So, make sure to taste the chiles.

The flavor of chiles changes once they are roasted and peeled—they aren't as sharp and vegetal—they aren't less hot or any hotter, but different, with a mellow, deep, richer heat. The heat mostly comes from the seeds and membranes, although the meat of the chile contains quite a bit, too.

Choose a chile that will be large enough to be appropriate for how you want to use it. For example, serrano chiles might have the right flavor profile for some of the poppers in this book, but they're just too small, which is why I use jalapeños.

There are three chiles that are primarily used for making rellenos: Anaheim, poblano, and jalapeño. For most of the year, the **Anaheim** is the mildest, except in the fall, when it can be quite spicy. It is also the lightest in color (almost lime green) and the longest, generally 6 to 8 inches long and ranging from about 1 to 1½ inches in diameter at the stem, tapering to a point. The **poblano** is a dark forest green, squatter than the Anaheim, about 5 inches long and 4 inches in diameter at the stem, with an almost triangular shape narrowing into a small, rounded tip. While the body of the Anaheim tends to be fairly straight-sided, the poblano is slightly misshapen, with valleys and small indentations in its body. The **jalapeño,** the smallest of the three chiles, is about 2 to 3 inches long and about $1/2$ to $3/4$ inch in diameter at the stem, tapering evenly and smoothly into a rounded tip. It is bright green and on a color chart would be about halfway between the greens of the Anaheim and the poblano. Poblanos tend to be a little spicier with a deeper, richer flavor. They are also larger and will hold more filling. The jalapeños are the smallest and hottest of the three, but they make great poppers because of their compact size and the punch they pack.

Dried chiles are rarely used for rellenos because the intensity can overpower the flavors in the fillings. Dried chiles also tend to be tougher and harder to cut and shape than fresh ones, making them difficult to work with and to eat.

HOW CHILES GET THEIR HEAT

There are hundreds of varieties of chiles, from excruciatingly hot like the habanero or chiltepín to the relatively mild Anaheim. The active ingredient in chiles that provides heat is a chemical called capsaicin. About 80 percent of the capsaicin is concentrated in the seeds and white membranes of the chiles and is dispersed in lesser quantities throughout the chile. When making rellenos, take care to remove the seed pod and as much of the white membrane as possible. This will moderate the heat and reduce the chances of burning out people's palates when they take that last bite near the stem and find it is full of seeds.

Preparing the Chiles

To prepare the chiles for stuffing you must remove their waxy outer skins, their seeds, and their membranes. There are several ways to remove the skins, and each technique will result in slightly different flavors and will yield firmer or softer chiles. As much as possible, you'll want to preserve the firmness of the flesh, or meat, of the chile so that it will hold the filling without falling apart or rupturing.

However, there is a trade-off. The techniques that yield the firmest flesh, don't, for the most part, add much flavor. Conversely, techniques that add flavor, such as roasting over an open fire, also tend to cook the meat of the chile, which makes it trickier to peel, and can leave chiles that are thin and torn, and that will easily rupture.

The firmness of the meat is directly related to the intensity of the heat source, the speed at which the skin blisters, and the rate at which the chiles can be cooled and peeled. The following techniques are listed in order of which technique yields the softest to firmest cooked and peeled chiles.

ROASTING CHILES OVER A FIRE
(Will yield the softest chiles)
Tools: long tongs; fire-resistant gloves; damp cloths, damp newspapers, brown paper bags, or ice water

In a barbeque or fire pit, build a fire with wood, charcoal briquets, or mesquite charcoal. The better and harder the wood, the hotter the fire will be. Fragrant woods like mesquite or pecan impart great flavors to the chiles. When the fire subsides and leaves a good coal base, toss as many chiles directly onto the fire as will reasonably fit. Using the tongs, turn the chiles as soon as they begin to blister and blacken, taking care to let them blacken all over. As soon as each chile is completely blistered, quickly remove it from the fire, place between the folds of damp cloths or newspapers, then seal in a paper bag for a couple of minutes, or toss directly in ice water. Using the cloth/newspapers/paper bag method is more traditional and will allow the chiles to steam a little bit, causing the skin to loosen. Using ice water effectively stops the cooking process quite quickly and helps keep the meat from overcooking. I generally use the ice water method, but purists may prefer the other techniques. In any case, after the chiles have cooled, use your fingers (with gloves, if you like) to peel the charred parts from the meat of the chile. With a sharp knife, make a slit the length of the chile from its stem to the tip. Then, using your fingers and a sharp knife, remove the seedpod, which is located near the stem, any remaining seeds, and as much of the white membrane as possible. If your fire is very

hot and the chiles are thick skinned, you will have chiles ready to stuff. If you find that the meat of the chile is too thin, or has ripped in several places, they will taste great but not make good candidates for stuffing. They will work well, however, in salsas, as rajas, or in recipes for chiles rellenos casseroles.

ROASTING CHILES OVER THE FLAMES OF A GAS BURNER
(Will yield slightly firmer chiles)
Tools: long tongs; high BTU gas grill; ice water

Place as many chiles as will fit comfortably directly on the flames of a gas burner. Using the tongs, turn the chiles as soon as they begin to blister and blacken, taking care to let them blacken all over. As soon as each chile is completely blistered, quickly remove it from the flames and submerge in the ice water for a minute or two before peeling.

PEELING CHILES IN A DEEP FRYER
(Will yield the second most firm chiles)
Tools: deep fryer; cooking deep-fat thermometer; long tongs; ice water

A commercial fryer works well if you have access to one, otherwise you can use a small tabletop appliance or set up a 1-gallon, thick-walled pot filled with 2½ quarts of canola or other neutral-flavored oil with a high flash point. With any of these tools, heat the oil to 375°F and slide as many chiles as will fit comfortably into the oil without it boiling over or losing too much heat. Make sure the chiles are dry as any moisture will cause the hot oil to pop and spit. The chiles will blister quite quickly in the oil. Using a pair of tongs, turn them often enough to make sure they are blistered on all sides, then pull the chiles from the oil and plunge them into ice water to stop their cooking. The skins will peel off quite easily, leaving very firm-fleshed chiles.

ROASTING CHILES WITH A PROPANE TORCH
(Will yield the firmest chiles)
Tools: propane torch; tongs or turning fork; damp towel

This is the slowest and most accurate method for peeling chiles. It imparts no flavor to the chile but leaves the thickest, meatiest skinless chile. Use a propane torch with the flame at its most focused setting. Working with one chile at a time, skewer each chile or hold it with tongs and hold the chile in the hottest part of the flame until it begins to blister and blacken. As the chiles blisters, move it through the flame. Once the entire chile is blistered you can easily rub off the skin with a damp towel.

For the any rellenos in this book, unless specifically mentioned in the recipe, use any of the last three peeling techniques for preparing your chiles. Using the equipment that's available to you, feel free to experiment with these methods until you find the one that's easiest and yields the best and most consistent results.

PREPARING THE CHILES FOR STUFFING

Once the chiles are peeled, prepare them for stuffing by making a slit down one side from the stem to the tip with a small, thin, sharp paring knife. Working carefully, using your fingers (if your hands are sensitive or you're working with particularly hot chiles, you may want to wear thin, food-handler gloves) and the knife, make the opening large enough so that you can cut the seedpod from where it is attached to the stem, carefully pulling it away from the membranes and sides of the chile. Remove any remaining seeds with your fingers or by rinsing gently under cold water. Pat the chiles dry. This will create a large pocket in which you will place your stuffing.

BATTERS, BREADINGS, AND CRUSTS

BATTERS, BREADINGS, AND CRUSTS

The Best Ways to Cook Rellenos

MOST PROFESSIONAL CHEFS and home cooks in the Southwest make rellenos with Anaheim chiles that are dipped into a whipped egg white–lightened batter and then fried. I've seen rellenos made with batter that is ladled into the frying pan like pancake batter, the relleno is laid in the batter, then more batter is spooned over the top. The relleno is fried like a flapjack, flipped, and finished in the pan. In these cases, the batter should get equal billing, and because it looked pretty fun, I created a recipe for a breakfast relleno filled with chorizo, eggs, and cheese, fried in pancake batter.

Many traditional rellenos, like some of those found in Oaxaca, are not battered at all, but baked directly in the oven and served with a light tomato sauce. Sometimes the chiles are left unpeeled when they are stuffed, then cooked in a hot skillet, allowing the skins to blister and slough off while they cook.

Over the years, I've developed a number of batters and breadings for the various rellenos I make at the restaurant. Generally, I like the lighter batters to let the flavors of more delicate and subtle ingredients come through; I use the coarser breadings as a foil against stronger flavors.

The procedure for flouring the jalapeños, dipping them in an egg and milk mixture (called an **egg wash**), then rolling in breadcrumbs is a basic breading procedure. The flour helps the egg and milk adhere to the chile, and the egg and milk provide a base to which the breadcrumbs cling. For this technique, it's important to make each coating as light as possible so the breading doesn't become thick or gummy.

The techniques for cooking rellenos are pretty straight-forward. Rellenos are fried, baked, griddled, or heated on a grill.

FRYING

Any recipes that call for batter means the rellenos will be fried. Frying provides quick, direct heat that sets the batter immediately into a light, crunchy exterior. At the proper temperature of 360° to 370°F, the oil is barely absorbed into the batter and the resulting relleno will be neither heavy nor greasy. If the oil is too cool, the batter will absorb the oil and it will be heavy, greasy, and unpalatable. If the oil is too hot, the batter will scorch and burn before the filling is hot.

Choosing the proper oil is as important as cooking at the proper temperature. You'll need to select an oil or a fat that can withstand temperatures of 350° to 370°F without smoking or breaking down. That leaves out whole butter because the butter solids will burn. Clarified butter will work but is expensive and high in saturated fats.

Generally, oils rendered from animals, such as lard, butter, bacon grease, and duck fat, are high in saturated fat, but they also have great flavor. Traditional Mexican rellenos recipes call for cooking in lard, providing much flavor as well as job security for your cardiologist. Certain vegetable oils, such as coconut oil, contain lots of saturated fats, virtually no flavor, and are definitely to be avoided. Canola and corn oils work well, are relatively low in saturated fats, inexpensive, and do not impart any flavor, which makes them good choices. Olive oil works well but is expensive and adds an unnecessary flavor profile. Grape seed oil is popular these days because of its clean flavor and high flash point. It is perfectly acceptable but more expensive than other options.

The best point of intersection in an imaginary flavor/health/economy/and utility graph can be reached by using canola oil in which you've fried corn tortillas to make homemade **corn tortilla chips**: Get some corn tortillas and cut them into 8 equal-sized pie-shaped wedges (see Corn Tortilla Crust, page 36). In the meantime, heat about 1 quart of canola oil to 350° to 370°F (use a deep-fat thermometer to monitor temperature) in a deep, 6-inch-diameter, thick-walled saucepot. Working in batches so as not to overcrowd or bring down the temperature of the oil, fry the chips for 1 to 2 minutes, until they're crunchy. Cool them on paper towels to absorb any excess oil. Lightly salt the chips and serve alone or with your favorite salsa. Now you've created a great snack and prepared your oil for cooking rellenos by imparting it with a great, slightly smoky, corn flavor. You can use the oil immediately or refrigerate it for up to about three weeks for later use.

When frying rellenos, use a cast-iron skillet or other thick-bottomed pan, and fill with oil about ¼-inch deep. Heat the oil to 350° to 370°F, monitoring the temperature with a deep-fat thermometer. After battering the rellenos one at a time, place as many as will fit comfortably in the pan, turning each relleno as the batter browns to a golden hue. In the course of the 3 to 4 minutes it will take to brown the relleno on all sides, the filling inside will heat through. To check this, insert a skewer or sharp knife into the center of the thickest part of the relleno for a couple of seconds, pull it out, and touch it to your wrist, cheek, nose, or other sensitive spot. If it's nice and hot, the relleno is ready. If not and the batter is properly cooked, as will happen with particularly thick or dense rellenos, place the rellenos in a 350°F oven for a couple of minutes until hot throughout. For those so equipped, an instant thermometer reading of 180°F will also tell you that the relleno is ready.

BAKING

Baking rellenos is limited to casseroles, delicate breading (which scorches in hot oil), and unbreaded, unbuttered rellenos. To bake rellenos, preheat the oven to 375°F and lighty grease or spray a baking sheet with nonstick spray. Place the rellenos on the baking sheet and cook for about 7 minutes, testing readiness as described above.

GRIDDLE OR GRILL COOKING

You can cook unbattered and unbreaded rellenos directly on a hot griddle. I've included a recipe from Zarela Martinez, the noted chef, restaurateur, and cookbook author who has been in the vanguard of popularizing authentic Mexican cuisine in the United States. She calls for unpeeled chiles in which the skins blister as the rellenos cook. This technique works equally well in a cast-iron skillet with a lid or on a barbecue with a cover. Place the rellenos on the hot, lightly greased surface and cover so that the inside of the chile will heat through. It will take 5 to 7 minutes to cook this way, and the benefit of this method, particularly when using the grill, is that the rellenos will take on some smoky flavor. Make sure you check the rellenos fairly frequently to ensure that they don't scorch on the bottom. If they do begin to scorch, either turn down the heat or move them to a cooler spot on the grill to finish cooking.

SAGUARO BLOSSOM SYRUP

Southern Arizona is the northernmost boundary for the slow-growing saguaro which doesn't begin to flower until about its thirtieth year. By late June the blossoms have dried and the fruit has begun to ripen. The saguaro harvest is an ancient practice that continues on Tohono O'odham lands much as it did centuries ago. Native American harvesters generally wait until nightfall to avoid the 100°F-plus temperatures of early July.

First, the ribs from the dried carcasses of long-dead cacti are gathered. These are fashioned into long poles, which are used to knock the fruit from the upper branches of the cactus; the fruits fall onto sacking that has been placed around the base of the plant. Although this procedure is repeated across many acres of cacti, it yields little fruit, and the syrup is scarcer still.

Next, a fire is made from gathered mesquite branches and the dried ribs of dead ocotillos and cholla cactus. A large *olla,* or clay pot, is filled with the ripe fruit and placed on the fire. Water captured from monsoon runoff is added to the boiling fruit, yielding a dark orange-colored juice. The juice is strained to separate the pulp, flowers, and any spines or dirt, and then returned to a clean pot to simmer and reduce until it is a sweet, thick, and a sticky, reddish-brown syrup known as *sitol*. Saguaro blossom syrup is available from Native Seeds SEARCH at (520) 622-5561.

Basic Beer Batter

This is our most basic and universal batter. It can be used for any of the rellenos because its flavor will not interfere with the fillings, and the slightly crisp crunchiness of fried beer batter plays wonderfully against the flesh of the chile. I like to use a light-bodied domestic beer. The purpose of the beer is for a little effervescence and yeastiness which lightens the batter, not for flavor.

BATTER FOR 4 TO 6 ANAHEIM RELLENOS

2 egg whites

1 whole egg

1 cup all-purpose flour

2 teaspoons olive oil

½ cup light beer

Beat the egg whites in a mixer until they form stiff peaks. Set aside.

In a stainless steel bowl, lightly beat the whole egg and slowly whip in ¾ cup of the flour and the olive oil, forming a thick, batter-like consistency. Whisk in the beer to form a slightly thick yet runny, lump-free liquid.

Fold in the egg whites and refrigerate for up to 30 minutes before using. The batter should be quite cold and the egg whites still light and airy when using.

To prepare the rellenos, roll them with the remaining ¼ cup flour, lightly shaking off any excess to help the batter adhere to the chile. Dip the chile into the batter so that each is well coated.

Cook the rellenos as directed.

Blue Cornmeal Breading

Blue cornmeal is now widely available in most grocery and specialty food stores. I often use it as a crust on rellenos that feature mushrooms because I like the way its light crunch and earthy flavor plays against the mushrooms. I use a slightly different breading technique with blue cornmeal because it tends to get gummy when applied with an egg wash. The reason we use more salt with the blue cornmeal than the panko is that the earthiness of the blue corn requires a little more to help bring out the flavor.

**BREADING FOR 4 TO 6 ANAHEIM RELLENOS,
2 TO 4 POBLANO RELLENOS,
OR 6 TO 8 JALAPEÑO POPPERS**

1 tablespoon kosher salt

2 cups blue cornmeal

2 egg whites

½ cup all-purpose flour

Combine the salt with the blue corn meal and set aside.

Beat the egg whites in a bowl until they just begin to form very soft peaks. Roll the prepared relleno in the flour, dusting off any excess, then dip the relleno into the egg whites to form a light coating, scraping off any excess with your fingers. Roll the relleno in the cornmeal, pressing lightly, to form a uniform, light coating.

Cook the rellenos as directed.

Pancake Batter

Use this batter with the breakfast rellenos or just by itself to make great, light pancakes. If using just for pancakes, fold in some fresh blueberries or strawberries, if available, just before serving.

BATTER FOR ABOUT 4 JUSTINO'S BREAKFAST RELLENOS (PAGE 52)

1½ cups flour

½ teaspoon salt

2½ teaspoons baking powder

1 egg

1 cup milk

3 tablespoons butter, melted

Sift the flour, salt, and baking soda together in a mixing bowl. In a separate bowl, whisk the egg, milk, and butter together, then gently stir into the dry ingredients. The batter will be lumpy, but don't overmix it.

Butter a large frying pan and heat over medium heat. Pour the batter 5 inches in diameter into the frying pan.

Lay a relleno across the center of the pancake and spoon a little more batter on top to coat the relleno. When the batter starts to bubble, flip the pancake and relleno and continue cooking for another minute or two, until the pancake is golden.

Panko Breading

Panko are the white, dried Japanese breadcrumbs that are available at most supermarkets or specialty food stores. They have a neutral flavor, are uniform in size, and crisp up nicely when used as breading. Panko crumbs are made by removing the crust from white bread, freezing the loaves, and then grating the still-frozen bread while air is blown across it.

BREADING FOR 4 TO 6 ANAHEIM RELLENOS, 2 TO 4 POBLANO RELLENOS, OR 6 TO 8 JALAPEÑO POPPERS

1 egg

¼ cup milk

½ cup all-purpose flour

1 cup panko crumbs

Pinch of kosher salt

Whisk the egg and milk together in a bowl and set aside. Combine the salt with the panko and set aside.

Roll the prepared rellenos in the flour, shaking off any excess. Dip the rellenos into the egg wash, allowing any excess egg to drip off, then roll them in the panko, pressing lightly to form a thin, uniform coating.

Cook the rellenos as directed.

Plantain Breading

Plantains come from southern Mexico, Central America, and the Caribbean and are a starchy cousin to bananas. When used as a breading, they form a very crunchy crust and impart a slightly nutty flavor. For this purpose, you will want green plantains that are quite firm, so that the carbohydrates have not yet begun to turn into sugar. Many plantain recipes call for very ripe plantains because they sweeten and soften as they ripen. The green plantains are not sweet at all and work perfectly for this recipe.

BREADING FOR 4 TO 6 ANAHEIM RELLENOS, 2 TO 4 POBLANO RELLENOS, OR 6 TO 8 JALAPEÑO POPPERS

2 quarts oil for frying (canola, grape seed, and corn oil all work well)

2 green (unripe) plantains

2 teaspoons kosher salt

2 eggs

¼ cup milk

1 cup all-purpose flour

Pour the oil into a large, deep pan, and preheat the oil to 350°F.

Peel the plantains. If the plantains are difficult to peel, use a knife to score the peel lengthwise in 3 or 4 places equidistant around the plantain. This will help you remove the peel.

Using a mandolin, a meat slicer, or a very sharp knife, slice the plantains lengthwise to about ⅛ inch thick. If the slices are too thin, they won't have enough flesh to grind into crumbs. If they are too thick, the surface of the plantains will burn before they are cooked in the center.

Working in batches so the temperature of the oil doesn't drop when the plantains are added and so that they do not overcrowd the pan, fry the plantains for 2 to 3 minutes in the oil, stirring them occasionally so they cook on all sides. The resulting plantains should be crunchy all the way through.

Cool the plantains on paper towels to soak up any excess oil. When the plantains have cooled, break them by hand into manageable pieces and, along with the salt, place them in a food processor fitted with a metal blade. Process until the plantains are uniformly coarsely ground. Be careful not to overprocess or the oils and starches will release and the plantains will become pasty. Transfer the mixture to a large plate.

In a separate bowl, beat the eggs with the milk.

Roll each prepared relleno in the flour, dusting off any excess, then dip into the egg wash, allowing any excess to drip off. Roll the prepared relleno in the plantain crumbs to form a thin, uniform crust.

Cook the rellenos as directed.

Tempura Batter

For a relleno that is more delicate in flavor, the cornstarch creates crunchiness, and the baking powder keeps it light.

BATTER FOR ABOUT 4 ANAHEIM RELLENOS

1½ teaspoons baking powder

½ cup cornstarch

1 cup all-purpose flour

1 egg yolk

2 cups ice water, or more as needed

Salt and white pepper

Combine the baking powder, cornstarch, ¾ cup of the flour, egg yolk, and ice water in a mixing bowl. Season with salt and white pepper.

To prepare the rellenos, roll them in the remaining ¼ cup flour, shaking off any excess. Dip the chile into the batter so that each is well coated.

Cook the rellenos as directed.

Corn Tortilla Crust

The flavor of fried tortillas is quite pronounced and makes a wonderfully crunchy crust that plays well with the flavors of certain rellenos.

CRUST FOR 4 TO 6 ANAHEIM RELLENOS, 2 TO 4 POBLANO RELLENOS, OR 6 TO 8 JALAPEÑO POPPERS

2 quarts oil for frying (canola, grapeseed, and corn oil all work well)

12 corn tortillas

2 teaspoons kosher salt

2 eggs

¼ cup milk

1 cup all-purpose flour

Pour the oil into a large, deep pan, and preheat the oil to 350°F.

Cut each tortilla into 8 wedges, as you might for a pie. Working in batches so the temperature of the oil doesn't drop, fry the tortillas for 1 to 2 minutes in the oil, stirring them occasionally so they cook evenly. The tortillas should be crunchy all the way through.

Remove the tortillas from the oil with a slotted spoon and let cool on paper towels to soak up excess oil. When the tortillas have cooled, break them by hand into manageable pieces and, along with the salt, place them in a food processor fitted with a metal blade. Process the tortillas until they are uniformly, coarsely ground. Be careful not to overprocess or the oils and starches will release and the tortillas will begin to become gummy. Transfer to a large plate.

Beat the eggs with the milk in a bowl. Roll each prepared relleno in the flour, dusting off any excess. Dip into the egg wash, allowing any excess to drip off, then roll them in the tortilla crumbs, pressing lightly to form a thin, uniform crust.

Cook the rellenos as directed.

UNTRADITIONAL, TRADITIONAL

CHEESE
CHILES
RELLENOS

Because cheese is the primary ingredient in many of traditional chiles rellenos, it's fun to play around with different varieties. I've included a few that I like, starting with a very simple classic. No matter which cheese you choose, when experimenting on your own, remember these keys for producing successful rellenos:

Make sure that the cheese has a high enough fat content to melt properly. Cheeses that are too dry will crumble but not melt; however, they can be blended with mild, fattier cheeses.

For a very strong relleno, Cotswold, the English Double Gloucester, is delicious. Any of the strong Cheddars work very well and, like the Cotswold, benefit from the addition of onions and chives.

Rich, creamy cheeses, such as Brie and Camembert, work quite well. Many goat and sheep's milk cheeses can be used, but sometimes they do not have enough fat to melt properly. In those cases, blend with a little cream cheese, Jack cheese, any other high-fat mild cheese, or even a little whole milk will work.

Various blue-veined cheeses such as Cabrales and Roquefort can be good, but I think they are too strong unless combined with other ingredients, as I've done in recipes such as Shrimp, Cabrales, and Chorizo Rellenos (page 67) and Cabrales, Bacon, and Chive Poppers in Panko Crust (page 94).

Many of the Mexican cheeses are excellent in rellenos. I've provided recipes that use Oaxacan cheese, queso fresco, and Panela, but many of the other fresh Mexican cheeses work very well.

Fresh mozzarella also makes great rellenos. It's stretchy and melts well, with a mild enough flavor that does not overpower other ingredients. I've included it in a recipe with wild mushrooms (page 68), but it is delicious on its own or blended with other ingredients.

Basic Monterey Jack Cheese Chiles Rellenos

For basic chiles rellenos, a mild, creamy cheese such as Monterey Jack, Oaxacan, or queso fresco is used, and the chiles are fire roasted before peeling, rather than by frying them to loosen the skin. The rellenos are then lightly floured and dipped into a simple egg batter for frying. This basic relleno is almost identical to the Chiles Rellenos Burrito "El Morro," the only difference is that, in this version, the chile is filled with more cheese to make it plumper.

4 RELLENOS

2 cups grated Monterey Jack

4 Anaheim chiles, fire roasted, seeded, and peeled

1 cup all-purpose flour

2 eggs lightly beaten with 2 ounces milk

2 tablespoons canola oil or other unflavored oil
   for frying

Divide the cheese into 4 equal portions, then stuff each of the chiles. Roll each of the rellenos in the flour, shaking off any excess, then dip each into the egg wash, allowing any excess egg to drip off.

Heat the oil in a hot griddle or cast-iron pan, and cook the chiles for about 2 minutes on each side, or until the cheese is melted.

Chiles Rellenos de Carne

Zarela Martinez provides this fragrant recipe in her book *The Food and Life of Oaxaca: Traditional Recipes from Mexico's Heart*. It works well with beef or pork and is both practical and economical as it uses up leftover roasted or stewed meats. The seasonings of cinnamon and cloves provide unusual flavors that are typical of Oaxaca. Shred the meat quite finely for a filling with a smooth consistency. Note that the batter used to coat the rellenos is simply beaten eggs.

6 RELLENOS

½ cup coarsely chopped blanched almonds

2 medium tomatoes

1½-inch piece cinnamon stick

3 tablespoons oil

1 medium yellow onion, finely diced

1 large clove garlic, minced

¼ teaspoon ground cloves

2 teaspoons minced fresh thyme leaves,
   or 1 teaspoon dried

½ cup raisins

2½ cups finely shredded cooked pork or beef

Salt and freshly ground black pepper

6 poblano chiles, prepared for stuffing (page 19)

1 cup unbleached flour

½ teaspoon salt

4 eggs, beaten

Vegetable oil for frying

Preheat the oven to 350°F.

Spread the almonds on a baking sheet and bake for about 10 minutes, until golden brown. Set aside.

Roast the tomatoes by blackening the skins on a hot griddle. Allow to cool slightly, and skin the tomatoes over a bowl to reserve the juices and pulp. Chop the tomatoes fine. Don't worry if you can't remove all the specks of black skin.

Grind the cinnamon stick with a mortar and pestle or in an electric coffee or spice grinder. Set aside.

In a skillet, heat the 3 tablespoons oil over medium-high heat until rippling. Add the onion and garlic and cook for 2 minutes, stirring often. Stir in the ground cinnamon, cloves, and thyme. Add the tomatoes and raisins and cook, stirring, for about 5 minutes. Add the shredded meat, cook for another 5 minutes, and season with salt and pepper to taste. Stir in the toasted almonds and let cool.

Carefully stuff the mixture into the chiles. Mix the flour with the salt and transfer to a wide bowl. Roll the prepared rellenos in the flour, then dip into the beaten egg.

Pour the vegetable oil into a large, heavy skillet 3 to 4 inches deep and heat to 375°F.

Slide 2 or 3 chiles at a time into the hot oil and fry. As the chiles turn golden, turn them to cook all sides evenly. Lift out and place on paper towels to absorb any excess oil.

Goat Cheese and Sun-Dried Tomato Rellenos with Golden Tomato Vinaigrette and Bread Salad

The combination of goat cheese, sun-dried tomatoes, and cilantro is immensely satisfying, and it is one I repeat in pastas and sandwiches as well as in rellenos. Served with the Bread Salad, it makes a light lunch or dinner.

4 RELLENOS

1 cup soft goat cheese

2 tablespoons milk

4 tablespoons roughly chopped, oil-packed sun-dried tomatoes

4 tablespoons chopped cilantro

2 tablespoons finely chopped scallions

4 Anaheim chiles, prepared for stuffing (page 19)

1 recipe Basic Beer Batter (page 30)

Vegetable oil for frying

1 recipe Golden Tomato Vinaigrette (page 125)

1 recipe Bread Salad (page 114)

Purée or blend the goat cheese with the milk so that it's soft and creamy. Fold in the sun-dried tomatoes, cilantro, and scallions. Divide the filling into quarters and carefully stuff the chiles. Dip in the beer batter and seal with toothpicks to help contain the stuffing.

Fill a large, heavy skillet with 1 inch of oil and heat to 375°F. Dip the chiles into the beer batter and fry until golden and the filling is hot. Finish in the oven if they turn too brown before the cheese is melted.

To serve, place 2 tablespoons of the Golden Tomato Vinaigrette on each plate. Place a relleno on the vinaigrette and the Bread Salad next to the relleno.

Holiday Apple and Walnut Rellenos

This recipe is a vegetarian variation of the Chiles en Nogado found in *Like Water for Chocolate* by Laura Esquivel. I use dried apples rather than fresh for stuffing because they have a more intense flavor and, with the juice from the grapes, fresh apples produce too much liquid. This is a great autumn and holiday dish because the flavors are festive and bright and the walnuts and apples signal the change of seasons.

4 RELLENOS

2 tablespoons corn oil

1/3 cup finely diced yellow onions

3 ounces dried apples, cut into small pieces

2 ounces cream cheese

Salt and pepper

4 ounces queso casero (or queso fresco or panela)

1 1/2 ounces walnut pieces, toasted

1/2 cup green grapes, cut in half lengthwise

4 Anaheim chiles, prepared for stuffing (page 19)

1 recipe Nogado (Walnut) Sauce (page 72)

1/4 cup pomegranate seeds

1 recipe Figs Stuffed with Roasted Walnuts, Queso Casero, and Agave Nectar (page 111)

Preheat the oven to 350°F.

Heat the oil in a sauté pan. Cook the onions with the apples, seasoning with salt and pepper, until the onions caramelize and the apples are soft, about 3 to 5 minutes.

Using an electric mixer, blend the cream cheese with the queso casero, then fold in the onion, apple, and walnut pieces by hand. Gently fold in the grape halves. Stuff the prepared chiles and wipe them clean.

Bake the chiles in the oven for about 5 minutes, until hot throughout.

Divide the sauce equally among four plates, and place a relleno on top of each. Sprinkle with pomegranate seeds and place a fig next to each relleno.

Calabacitas con Queso Rellenos

This combination of calabacitas (baby squash, or in this case, diced zucchini), cheese, corn, and tomatoes is often prepared as a side dish. Stuffed into roasted poblano chiles, it makes a wonderful and flavorful main course when served with Black Beans and Green Rice.

4 RELLENOS

2 tablespoons corn oil, or enough to coat pan

½ cup chopped yellow onion

2 tablespoons chopped garlic

1½ cups diced zucchini or yellow squash

¾ cup sweet corn kernels

4 tablespoons peeled, seeded, and diced Anaheim chiles

½ cup roughly chopped tomatoes

Salt and pepper

1½ cups crumbled queso fresco

4 poblano chiles, prepared for stuffing (page 19)

2 ounces fresh cilantro leaves

Preheat the oven to 400°F.

Heat the oil in a sauté pan over medium-high heat. Add the onion, and sauté for about 1 minute, until they just begin to soften. Add the garlic, zucchini, corn, and Anaheim chiles, and sauté for 4 to 5 minutes, stirring constantly, until the zucchini becomes fairly soft. Add the tomatoes and cook another 4 minutes, stirring constantly. The zucchini and tomatoes will give off a fair amount of water, making the mixture a little wet. Season with salt and pepper.

Let the mixture cool, then fold in 1 cup of the queso fresco. Stuff the rellenos and bake in the oven for about 10 minutes, until the rellenos are very hot in the center.

Remove from the oven, and sprinkle the remaining ½ cup queso fresco and the cilantro leaves on the rellenos. Serve with Green Rice and Black Beans.

Cuitlacoche, Queso Fresco, Corn, Sun-Dried Tomato, and Chipotle Morita Rellenos

Cuitlacoche is a fungus that grows on corn, engorging the kernels to several times their normal size and turns them charcoal black. Long considered a nuisance in the U.S., cuitlacoche is prized in Mexico, where it is served in quesadillas, sauces, and soups. Canned cuitlacoche can be found in Mexican specialty markets or online. I often pair it with corn to show the contrasts and color, but I also use it to make cold soups, vinaigrettes, and relishes. The chipotle morita is the dry-smoked jalapeño. It is very hot, with an intense, smoky flavor so use it sparingly.

4 RELLENOS

2 tablespoons corn oil

6 ounces fresh, sweet corn kernels

1 teaspoon chopped fresh garlic

Freshly ground black pepper

1/8 teaspoon chipotle morita, reconstituted in water and finely chopped

2 ounces oil-packed sun-dried tomatoes, chopped

6 ounces cuitlacoche, canned or fresh

6 ounces queso fresco, crumbled

2 ounces fresh cilantro leaves

4 poblano chiles, prepared for stuffing (page 19)

Preheat the oven to 400°F.

Coat a small sauté pan with the corn oil and sauté the corn kernels and garlic over medium heat for about 3 minutes, until the corn starts to soften and the garlic releases its flavor. Season with freshly ground pepper.

Remove from the heat and transfer to a bowl. Fold in the chipotle morita, sun-dried tomatoes, and cuitlacoche and mix well. Gently fold in the queso fresco and cilantro. Stuff the poblanos with the filling.

Place in the oven and bake for 10 minutes, until very hot in the center. Serve with Guacamole, Roasted Corn Vinaigrette, and Chiltepín Salsa.

Justino's Breakfast Rellenos

I created this relleno in honor of my buddy, Justin Turner, a hydrologist by trade who probably never thought he would be mentioned in a cookbook. One evening, sitting around the table, as we were having a cocktail with our wives, I was telling them about my plans for this book. To the surprise of all of us, Justin, who had done some baking earlier in his life but whose main attribute in the kitchen is washing dishes, described *his* chile relleno this way:

"Take a chile out of a can and stuff it with any kind of cheese, doesn't matter. Then make a batter out of a couple of eggs, separate them, whip the whites and fold in some flour. Make a pancake out of the batter, then lay the relleno in the middle of the pancake, put some more batter on top of the chile, then flip it. Now that's a relleno!"

I'm sure Justin won't mind that I've embellished his relleno a bit by stuffing the chiles with chorizo and eggs and cooking them in pancake batter.

4 RELLENOS

4 ounces spicy ground chorizo

1 ounce yellow onion, finely diced

2 eggs, beaten

3 ounces Cheddar cheese, grated

4 Anaheim chiles, prepared for stuffing (page 19)

2 tablespoons clarified butter

1 recipe Pancake Batter (page 32)

2 tablespoons saguaro blossom syrup
  (maple syrup may be substituted)

In a large frying pan, preferably cast-iron, over medium heat, fry the chorizo and the onion for 3 to 4 minutes, or until the chorizo is cooked. Remove the chorizo and most of the fat from the pan, pour the eggs into the frying pan, and scramble.

When they start to firm up but are still quite moist, fold in the chorizo and Cheddar and remove from the heat. When the eggs are cooked enough to handle, stuff them into the chiles. Pull the rellenos tight to seal in the stuffing.

Wipe the frying pan clean, add the clarified butter, and heat over medium heat.

Ladle a 6-inch-diameter circle of pancake batter into the middle of the pan. Place a relleno in the middle of the pancake and spoon more batter over the relleno. When the batter starts to bubble, flip the pancake and the relleno and continue cooking for another minute or two, until the pancake is golden brown. Transfer to a warm oven while you make the remaining relleno pancakes.

Drizzle with a little saguaro blossom syrup and serve immediately.

Lobster and Black Bean Rellenos with Champagne Sauce

Sometimes it's fun (and tasty) to combine elegant, luxurious ingredients with those that might be considered slightly more humble. In this relleno, I've taken freshly cooked lobster meat and combined it with black beans and chipotles in adobo, which I serve on a rich, lobster-scented champagne sauce at the restaurant. Chipotles in adobo can be found in Mexican markets as well as most supermarkets. They are dry-smoked jalapeños that have been prepared in a marinade of vinegar, tomato, and garlic. They are quite hot, but here their heat is balanced by the black beans, and both play well against the rich lobster.

4 RELLENOS

6 ounces lobster meat, cooked

$1/2$ cup chopped scallions

$1/2$ cup cooked, rinsed black beans

$1/2$ teaspoon chopped chipotle in adobo

1 teaspoon chopped garlic

3 ounces cream cheese

3 ounces queso blanco

4 Anaheim chiles, prepared for stuffing (page 19)

Oil for frying

1 recipe Basic Beer Batter (page 30)

1 recipe Champagne Sauce (page 134)

Cut the lobster meat into large nuggets about $3/4$ inch per side and toss with the scallions, black beans, chipotle, and garlic.

Blend the cream cheese and the queso blanco together, and fold the lobster mixture thoroughly into the cheese. Divide into 4 parts, and stuff into the chiles.

Fill a large, heavy skillet with 1 inch of oil and heat to 375°F. Dip the chiles into the beer batter and fry until golden and the filling is hot. Finish in the oven if they turn too brown before the cheese is melted. Serve with 2 tablespoons of sauce pooled under each relleno.

HOW TO COOK AND PREPARE
LOBSTER

To yield about 6 ounces of meat you will need two 1-pound lobsters. Combine 2 gallons of water with about 1/2 cup of salt and bring to a rapid boil. Plunge the live lobsters into the water and let them cook for 4 minutes. Cooking for this brief amount of time will leave the lobster meat very soft and tender. Remove the lobsters from the water and let them cool a little bit until you can handle them with a towel without burning yourself. Wrapping the towel around the lobster, twist the tail from the body and remove the claws.

Using a heavy knife, cut off the tail fins where they join the body. This will allow you to remove the tail meat in one piece by pushing the meat out of the tail shell with your finger; push from the bottom of the tail toward the end removed from the stomach. To remove the claw meat, use a 1½-inch-diameter wooden dowel, the dull side of a heavy knife, or a hammer. Place a towel over the claws to keep the juices from splattering, and strike the shells with quick, sharp taps. Don't pound the claws or you will shatter the shells and embed them into the smashed meat. The goal is to crack the shell just enough so that you can remove it with your fingers and the meat can be extracted intact. To remove the meat from the knuckles, poke it out with the sharp end of one of the claws.

Once the meat is removed, cut into large nuggets about 3/4 inch per side.

Reserve the shells and the body for Lobster Stock.

Lobster and Brie Rellenos with Nantua Sauce

This elegant relleno is the first relleno I ever made. It was 1987, and I was experimenting with blending French influences with the flavors of the Southwest. I wanted to create a relleno that was at once rich and decadent but still had a bite from the chile that would create a counterpoint for the luxurious textures and flavors of the filling. For this dish you can use whole, live lobsters or frozen cold-water lobster tails.

Jicama is a tuber with a rough, brown skin that must be removed. The meat of the jicama is white and crunchy, with lots of moisture and a cool, refreshing flavor that offers an excellent counterpoint to this rich relleno.

4 RELLENOS

Olive oil to coat bottom of small sauté pan

6 ounces lightly cooked lobster meat (page 55), roughly chopped

$1/2$ teaspoon chopped chipotle in adobo

1 teaspoon chopped garlic

$1/4$ cup diced scallions

Salt and freshly ground black pepper

1 tablespoon brandy

1 tablespoon Pernod

3 ounces triple-crème Brie

3 ounces cream cheese

4 Anaheim chiles, prepared for stuffing (page 19)

Vegetable oil for frying

1 recipe Basic Beer Batter (page 30)

1 recipe Nantua (Lobster) Sauce (page 132)

1 recipe Jicama Slaw (page 109)

continued

Heat a sauté pan with the olive oil, and lightly sauté the lobster meat with the chipotle, garlic, scallions, salt, and pepper over medium to low heat for about 2 minutes to marry the flavors. Add the brandy and Pernod. If you're cooking on a gas stove, *carefully* tip the pan slightly until the liquid catches fire, and continue cooking until the flames subside, just a few seconds. Otherwise, ignite the brandy and Pernod with matches or a lighter. In either case, be careful not to lean toward the pan while lighting.

Blend the Brie and cream cheese together. Fold in the lobster and mix thoroughly. Stuff the mixture into the roasted Anaheim chiles.

Fill a large, heavy skillet with 1 inch of vegetable oil and heat to 375°F. Dip the chiles into the beer batter and fry until golden, about 2 minutes per side. Finish in the oven until the cheese is melted, if necessary.

Pool the sauce on four plates, place a relleno on top, and garnish with the Jicama Slaw.

Mango, Apple, and Roquefort Rellenos

I created this relleno when one of my cooks, Neal Swidler, returned from a trip to France with a bottle of Sauternes for me. I wanted to create a dish to honor his gift and the great flavors of the wine while keeping within the genre of the cooking we had been doing together. Apples and Roquefort are tried and true complements to Sauternes, and I believed the mango, with its unique tropical flavor, would add a little twist that would help bring out the flavors of the wine. Mango Coulis helps to bolster the mango flavor in the relleno, and the Green-Apple Pecan Salad adds another crunchy dimension to the dish. When this recipe is paired with the Figs Wrapped in Serrano Ham, these rellenos take on a whole new level of texture and harmonious flavor combinations.

4 RELLENOS

1 ripe mango, peeled

1 Granny Smith apple, peeled

3 ounces Roquefort or other deeply-veined blue cheese

1½ ounces cream cheese

4 Anaheim chiles, prepared for stuffing (page 19)

Flour for dusting

1 recipe Basic Beer Batter (page 30)

Vegetable oil for frying

6 ounces Mango Coulis (page 135)

6 ounces Green Apple–Pecan Salad (page 120)

4 Figs Wrapped in Serrano Ham with Whole Roasted Almonds and Roquefort (page 112)

Slice the mango into ⅛-inch-wide strips. Dice the apple into small pieces. Blend the Roquefort and cream cheese in a bowl. Fold the apple into the blended cheese. Pipe or place the Roquefort and apple mixture into each chile. Place 3 or 4 strips of mango next to the cheese, using toothpicks to seal the chile shut.

Lightly flour the chiles and dip into the beer batter.

Fill a large, heavy skillet with 1 inch of oil and heat to 375°F. Fry the chiles, turning, until golden brown on all sides, about 3 minutes per side.

Ladle 1½ ounces of coulis onto each of four plates. Place a relleno on top of the sauce. Garnish with the Apple-Pecan Salad and serve with the Figs Wrapped in Serrano Ham.

Lamb Barbacoa

In Oaxaca they make sensational barbacoa by marinating the lamb in a very fragrant blend of chiles, herbs, and spices, then pit-roasting it for several hours until it is fork-tender and falls easily from the bones. I developed this recipe so that I can roast the lamb in the oven. The flavors are extremely aromatic and I like to serve the rellenos with the Mushroom Escabèche to let the acid from the pickled mushrooms cut through the richness of the lamb.

This recipe will yield enough to make two meals from the lamb. For the first, make the following recipe for the barbacoa, serving it with the soup made from the pan juices as a first course, which is how it is served in Oaxaca. I've included recipes for some Frijoles de la Olla, which are simply cooked pinto beans and Orange-Jicama Salad, a great accompaniment to the lamb. Use the leftover lamb for the the rellenos. It freezes well and is a great party dish.

Note: You'll want to use meat that is a little fatty because it will add to the richness of the dish. I'd advise against using rack of lamb not only because it's expensive, but because it will not benefit from the long cooking process.

ABOUT 5 POUNDS COOKED MEAT

6 ounces guajillo chiles (about 8 large chiles),
   tops and seeds removed

1 quart boiling water

3 teaspoons cumin seeds

1 tablespoon whole cloves

16 allspice berries

3 tablespoons dried Mexican oregano, crumbled

10 large sprigs fresh thyme

20 cloves garlic

2 large onions, coarsely chopped

2 cups cider vinegar

2 teaspoons salt plus more for seasoning

Freshly ground black pepper

8-pound bone-in or 6-pound boneless lamb leg,
   or 6 pounds lamb stew meat

4 ounces dried avocado leaves (or 1 tablespoon
fennel seed, ground with the cumin, cloves and
allspice can be substituted)

Frijoles de le Olla (page 106)

Orange Jicama Salad (page 116)

Toast the dried guajillo chiles on a hot dry griddle for a couple of minutes, turning them frequently with tongs so they don't scorch. Soak the toasted chiles in the boiling water.

Grind the cumin seeds, cloves, and allspice with a mortar and pestle or in an electric coffee or spice grinder.

Drain the soaked chiles, reserving the liquid (for this recipe and to make the soup, page 64). Working in batches if necessary, place them in a blender with the ground spices, oregano, garlic, onion, vinegar, the 2 teaspoons of salt, and about ½ cup of the soaking liquid. Process to a smooth purée, stopping occasionally to scrape down the sides with a rubber spatula.

Season the lamb with salt and pepper. Slather the seasoning paste all over the meat. Arrange in a large bowl (or any nonreactive container that's large enough), cover tightly with plastic wrap, and refrigerate overnight or for at least 4 hours. Remove from the refrigerator, and allow the meat to come to room temperature before cooking; this could take up to 2 hours.

Preheat the oven to 325°F.

Choose a deep roasting pan or baking dish that is large enough to hold the meat snugly. Scatter half the avocado leaves and half the fresh thyme on the bottom of the pan and arrange the meat on top. Scatter the remaining half of the avocado leaves and thyme over the meat.

Cover the pan (or wrap very tightly with several layers of foil if there is no lid) and bake for 6 to 7 hours. The meat should be completely cooked throughout and very tender, almost falling off the bone. If using lamb stew meat it will begin to fall apart. If using bone-in or boneless leg of lamb it shred quite easily.

continued

Remove the meat from the pan along with about half the roasting juices and residue and reserve for reheating with the lamb. Leave the remainder of the juices and residue in the roasting pan to make the soup. Let the lamb cool enough so that you can handle it. Remove any large pieces of avocado leaf, if any remain. Shred the meat fairly coarsely. It can be easily reheated by warming it slowly in its own juices.

Oaxacan Lamb Barbacoa Rellenos

You're going to enjoy the Lamb Barbacoa recipe so much that you may be tempted to eat it all, leaving no leftovers for the relleno. Try to resist the temptation, or just make a bigger batch to start with. I guarantee you'll love how the barbacoa tastes in a relleno. Serve the rellenos with Mushroom Escabache, Frijoles de la Olla or Black Beans, and Green Rice for a wonderfully complete meal. A nice cold beer or margarita would go down pretty well, too.

4 RELLENOS

3 cups shredded Lamb Barbacoa (page 60)

4 poblano chiles, prepared for stuffing (page 19)

1 tablespoon canola oil

$^1/_2$ cup queso fresco

Preheat the oven to 375°F.

Divide the lamb into four servings and stuff into the chiles.

Brush a little oil onto an ovenproof pan and brush the remainder onto the outside of the stuffed chiles. Heat the rellenos in the oven for about 10 minutes, until the meat is quite hot in the center, then sprinkle with the queso fresco and put back in the oven for another 3 minutes so that the cheese begins to brown slightly.

Leftover Lamb Barbacoa Soup

A by-product of making the Lamb Barbacoa, the traditional way to make this soup is to capture the drippings by setting a pot under the lamb as it roasts in the pit. This recipe is a does a great job of recreating those flavors.

ABOUT 1 QUART

Roasting juices and residue from roasting pan (pages 60–61)

$1/2$ cup chopped carrots

$1/2$ cup chopped onions

$1/2$ cup chopped celery

2 guajillo chiles, stemmed, seeded, and torn into pieces

2 tablespoons tomato paste

$3^1/2$ cups water from the soaked chiles (pages 60-61)

2 cups water

1 recipe Lamb Barbacoa (page 60)

Place the roasting pan in which the lamb was cooked on the stovetop over medium heat. Add the carrots, onions, celery, and chiles, and cook for a few minutes, stirring constantly, to soften the vegetables.

Stir in the tomato paste, then deglaze the pan with the reserved chile water, scraping up all the particles and residue from the roasted lamb.

Add the 2 cups water and bring to a boil, then lower the heat and bring the liquid to a slow simmer, cooking for about 30 minutes.

Remove from the heat and strain. Pick out any large pieces of chiles and any large pieces of avocado leaf that remain and return the vegetables to the broth.

In the meantime, toast the guajillo chiles on a hot dry pan, turning once, for 2 to 3 minutes total, to bring out their oils and flavor. Then add to the lamb broth.

Serve the soup alongside the lamb or as a first course.

Chiles Verdes Rellenos

This recipe is from Zarela Martinez's *The Food and Life of Oaxaca: Traditional Recipes from Mexico's Heart*. Martinez notes that the secret to the flavor in this relleno is the home-rendered lard; store-bought lard is the next best option, followed by bacon grease, which is delicious but not authentic. To make this dish vegetarian, though also not authentic, brown a little freshly crushed garlic and chile powder in 4 tablespoons of butter instead of the lard or bacon fat. Let the butter cool and solidify. In Martinez's recipe, the chiles are served unpeeled and left to the diner to peel before eating.

8 RELLENOS

8 fresh Anaheim chiles

4 tablespoons home-rendered lard or bacon fat

Pinch of salt

24 ounces queso fresco, crumbled

2 tablespoons fresh epazote leaves stripped from the
    stem, or 2 teaspoons crumbled dried epazote

Cut a shallow, 1½-inch incision lengthwise into the side of each chile and carefully scrape out the seeds without tearing the chile.

Scoop up ½ tablespoon of fat and spread generously in the interior of each chile, then sprinkle the fat with a little salt. Fill each chile with some of the cheese and epazote and squeeze the chile shut.

Heat a griddle or cast-iron skillet over high heat. Griddle-roast the chiles until blackened on all sides, using tongs to turn and hold them shut as necessary to keep the filling from oozing out.

Martinez serves the rellenos with Caldillo de Tomate.

Shrimp, Cabrales, and Chorizo Rellenos with Andalusian Gazpacho Sauce

This recipe uses blue-veined Spanish Cabrales cheese and spicy Spanish chorizo from Los Palacios. The gazpacho sauce is based on a recipe from Andalusia.

4 RELLENOS

6 large Guaymas shrimp

2 teaspoons butter

4 tablespoons finely diced Spanish chorizo

2 teaspoons freshly crushed garlic

5 ounces Cabrales cheese

5 ounces cream cheese

4 tablespoons minced scallions

4 Anaheim chiles, prepared for stuffing (page 19)

1 cup all-purpose flour

Egg wash (page 26)

Plantain and corn tortilla crumbs (pages 34 and 36)

1 recipe Andalusian Gazpacho Sauce (page 127)

Chop the shrimp into ¼-inch pieces. Melt the butter in a hot skillet and lightly sauté the shrimp with the chorizo. After about 1 minute, add the garlic so that it will release its flavor without scorching. Cook the shrimp until it is just translucent but not completely cooked. It will finish cooking inside the relleno. Cooked this way, the chorizo will release some of its oil coating and coloring the shrimp, imbuing it with a spicy, rich flavor.

Blend the Cabrales, cream cheese, and scallions by hand. Fold in the shrimp and chorizo, and any oil from the chorizo and butter. Stuff the rellenos with the mixture.

Dust the chiles with flour, coat with egg wash, and encrust with a mixture of plantain and tortilla crumbs. Fry or bake as desired.

Pour about 2 ounces of sauce in the center of each plate and place a relleno on the sauce. With a spoon, layer the chopped gazpacho vegetables into a mound beside the rellenos.

Wild Mushroom and Madeira Rellenos

I celebrate the fall harvest of foraged chanterelle and lobster mushrooms by making these rich, sophisticated rellenos. In the spring and summer, I use morels and porcinis.

4 RELLENOS

$^1/_2$ pound chanterelle mushrooms

$^1/_2$ pound lobster mushrooms

3 tablespoons finely chopped shallots

1 tablespoon finely chopped garlic

2 cups dry white wine

Kosher salt and freshly ground pepper

$^1/_4$ cup chiffonaded fresh basil

$^1/_2$ cup diced fresh mozzarella

4 Anaheim chiles, prepared for stuffing (page 19)

1 recipe Tempura Batter (page 35)

Madeira Sauce (page 134)

Oil for frying

Roughly chop the mushrooms and combine with the shallots and garlic; place in a small, noncorrosive saucepot.

Cover with the white wine and reduce until the mushrooms are almost entirely dry. Season lightly with salt and pepper. Let the mushrooms cool, and fold in the basil and mozzarella. Divide into 4 portions, and stuff into the chiles.

Preheat the oven to 350°F. Dip each relleno into the batter and cover completely, except for the stems.

In a large pan, heat the oil until hot, but not smoking, and place the rellenos in the pan, allowing plenty of room to turn the rellenos. Cook in batches if necessary.

Cook the rellenos for 1 to 2 minutes per side without letting the batter scorch. Transfer to a baking sheet and finish in the oven for about 5 minutes.

Puddle some of the Madeira Sauce onto each plate and place a relleno on the sauce.

MUSHROOM FORAGERS

Sometimes, when you first get up in the morning, you just don't know how good your day will get. But when Dick Gruey decides to pay me a visit, my day starts to get a lot better.

Dick is a short, wiry fellow, with long, brown, out-of-control curly hair, just now tinged with grey, one of the biggest, bushiest beards you'll ever see, and eyes that sparkle when he arrives bearing gifts. Amongst other things, Dick forages mushrooms. If you ever have to guess what a mushroom forager might look like, you would picture Dick.

Years ago, one fall day when we were in our downtown restaurant, Dick appeared at the kitchen door after the lunch rush. We'd never met, nor had I ever heard of him. Seems he'd been up in the White Mountains of Arizona, about 150 miles north of us, and had collected some mushrooms he wanted to sell. Out of various brown paper bags came lobster mushrooms, some early chanterelles, and some boletus.

At the time I was still fairly new to Tucson and had no idea that mushrooms even existed in Arizona. So Dick and his brown paper bags filled with new treasures were a major surprise.

We all know eating wild mushrooms can be a scary, even deadly proposition, so as excited as I was, I knew I was out of my element. "Alright, Dick, we're going to eat 'em together," I said as I placed some sauté pans on the stove, crushed a little garlic, grabbed a bottle of brandy, some basil, cream and whatever else that came to hand. Dick and I had a feast that afternoon—and evening and, for the next few days, so did my guests.

Dick doesn't drop by all that frequently, in fact sometimes it can be years between visits. So I get a lot of my foraged mushrooms from some terrific guys up in Oregon. Dick's the most fun though, because every time he comes through the door with a twinkle in his eye and those bags full of mushrooms, everything else in the kitchen stops.

Chiles en Nogado

This is one of Mexico's legendary rellenos, and the recipe comes from *The Cusines of Mexico* by Diana Kennedy, who has been studying, authenticating, and popularizing regional Mexican cooking for several decades. It is said to have been created for a banquet honoring Don Agustín de Iturbide, who led the final revolt against Spain and signed the Treaty of Cordoba on August 28, 1821, giving Mexico her independence. All the dishes at the celebratory banquet represented the colors of the Mexican flag. In this relleno, the green chiles, white walnut sauce, and red pomegranates echo those national colors.

The end of August coincides with the Mexican walnut harvest, the beginning of pomegranate season, and the start of the chile harvest. In addition to being a dish of celebration and passion, it illustrates how seasonal ingredients are used to create new dishes.

Note: You will need to make the Nogado Sauce 1 day ahead.

6 RELLENOS

6 poblano chiles, prepared for stuffing (page 19)

1 recipe Stuffing (recipe follows)

2 cups Nogado Sauce (recipe follows),
   at room temperature

1 small bunch Italian parsley

Seeds of 1 small pomegranate

Stuff the chiles with the filling. Cover most of each chile with the sauce, leaving some of the relleno exposed.

Garnish with the parsley and pomegranate seeds.

Stuffing

1/2 pound Picadillo (recipe follows)

1/2 medium onion, finely chopped.

3 cloves garlic, peeled and chopped

6 tablespoons lard or fat reserved from the picadillo broth (page 73)

8 peppercorns, ground

5 whole cloves, ground

1/2-inch stick cinnamon, ground

3 tablespoons raisins

2 tablespoons blanched and slivered almonds

2 tablespoons chopped candied fruit

2 teaspoons salt

11/4 pounds tomatoes, peeled and seeded

1 pear, peeled and chopped

1 peach, peeled and chopped

Sauté the picadillo, onions, and garlic in the lard.

Fold in the peppercorns, cloves, cinnamon, raisins, almonds, candied fruit, salt, tomatoes, chopped pear, and chopped peach, and cook over medium heat for about 30 minutes, stirring frequently so the mixture doesn't scorch.

Remove from the heat and reserve for stuffing the rellenos.

continued

Picadillo

Picadillo is meat that has been cooked with vegetables and minced or ground. It often has onions and tomatoes and is used as a stuffing, as it is in this case.

ABOUT ½ POUND COOKED MEAT

¾ pound boneless pork butt, cut into 1-inch cubes

¼ onion, sliced

1 clove garlic, peeled

1 teaspoon salt

Place the meat in a saucepan, along with the onion, garlic, salt, and enough cold water to cover. Bring to a boil, lower the heat, and let simmer until tender, about 1½ hours. Do not overcook.

Let the meat cool in the broth. Once cooled, strain the meat, reserving the broth.

Shred or chop the meat finely and set aside. Let the broth get completely cold, then skim off and reserve the fat.

Nogado (Walnut) Sauce

3 CUPS

25 fresh walnuts, shelled

1 cup milk

1 small piece white bread, without crust

¼ cup queso fresco

1½ cups sour cream

½ teaspoon salt

Large pinch of powdered cinnamon

One day ahead, cover the walnuts with boiling water for about 5 minutes and then remove and peel the paper skin from the walnuts. Cover the walnuts in the milk and refrigerate overnight.

The next day, combine the walnuts in milk with the bread, queso fresco, sour cream, salt, and cinnamon in a food processor or blender. Purée all the ingredients.

Chiles Rellenos Burrito "El Morro"

My friend Randy Spalding, a special education instructor at Pueblo High School, spends his summers traveling the world and sending dispatches back from Internet cafes along the way. His e-mails invariably begin with, "You won't believe what I had for dinner last night. . . ."

For years, Randy's been telling me about the Chiles Rellenos Burritos at El Morro Restaurant in Nogales, Sonora. And when he made them for Rebecca and me one night, it confirmed our need to try the original.

Once you unwrap the tortilla and slather it with silky Refried Beans and Spicy Pico de Gallo, then rewrap it, you'll realize the tortilla exists to pack more goodness around the relleno.

4 RELLENO BURRITOS

1 cup queso fresco

4 Anaheim chiles, prepared for stuffing (page 19)

1 cup all-purpose flour

2 eggs

4 tablespoons milk

4 (12-inch) flour tortillas

1 recipe Spicy Pico de Gallo (page 137)

1 recipe Refried Beans (page 105)

Divide the cheese into 4 equal portions, then stuff each of the chiles. Roll each of the rellenos in the flour, shaking off any excess.

Beat the eggs and milk together. Dip each of the rellenos into the egg mixture to lightly coat them, letting any excess egg drip off.

Lightly oil a griddle or cast-iron pan, heat the pan, then add the rellenos and cook for about 2 minutes on each side, until the cheese is melted.

In the meantime, heat the tortillas and distribute among four plates. When the rellenos are cooked, place one in the center of each tortilla and wrap, tucking in the ends.

Serve immediately with the Pico de Gallo and Refried Beans so the rellenos remain very hot and the tortillas don't become soggy.

Toritos "La Roca"

For almost thirty years, La Roca Restaurant in Nogales, Sonora, has been a family favorite of ours. Opened by the Wilson-Bohn family, La Roca (the rock) is built into a hillside, which forms one wall of the elegant dining room. Although this makes a great backdrop, I go to La Roca for the food. With unique dishes like these toritos, La Roca is a treasure.

8 RELLENOS

2 cups, plus 3 tablespoons olive oil

8 yellow caribe chiles

6 tablespoons soy sauce

8 medium raw shrimp, peeled and deveined

4 thin slices bacon, cut in half

Pink grapefruit supremes, for garnish

In a deep skillet, heat the 2 cups of olive oil over medium-high heat to 375°F. Fry the chiles in the olive oil, turning them occasionally, until they are completely blistered. Remove from the oil, and place in the folds of a damp towel for a few minutes until the skins peel off easily. Peel the chiles, cut a slit lengthwise into each, and remove the seeds and seedpods.

Put the soy sauce and the remaining 3 tablespoons of olive oil in a small saucepan. Simmer the whole shrimp for a minute or two, until they are not quite cooked through.

Remove from the pan and chop each shrimp into 3 or 4 pieces. Return the pieces to the soy sauce and olive oil and cook a little longer, until the shrimp are completely cooked but not overcooked.

Stuff each chile with 3 or 4 pieces of shrimp, and wrap with a piece of bacon, securing with a toothpick. Heat a skillet and pan-sear the rellenos for 3 or 4 minutes, turning once, until the bacon is completely cooked but not too crisp.

Serve with the soy sauce and olive oil as a dipping sauce and garnish with the grapefruit supremes.

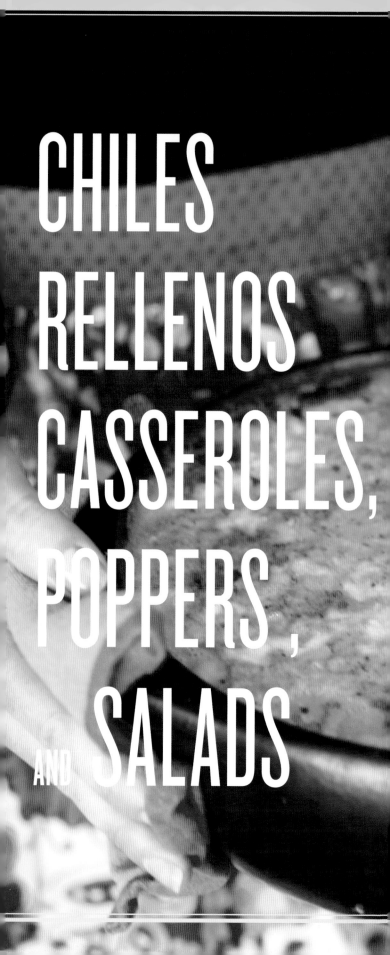

CHILES RELLENOS CASSEROLES, POPPERS, AND SALADS

Verduras Chiles Rellenos Casserole

The combination of chiles, corn, and sweet potatoes, along with the smoky flavors from grilled zucchini, eggplant, and mushrooms, make this an immensely satisfying dish. Creating a casserole allows for the layering of the ingredients in a way that wouldn't work as well in a stuffed relleno. Serve with a salad of *verdolagas* (page 119), the greens also known as purslane, which grow wild in the arroyos and washes in the Southwest after it rains.

SERVES 6 TO 8

8 Anaheim chiles, roasted, seeded, and peeled

4 tablespoons olive oil, or more as needed

3 tablespoons finely chopped fresh garlic

2 teaspoons kosher salt

1 teaspoon freshly ground black pepper

1 eggplant, peeled and sliced into ¾-inch-thick rounds

3 zucchini, sliced lengthwise ¼ inch thick

4 portobello mushrooms, gills removed

2 cups fresh corn removed from the cob

2 cups peeled and diced sweet potato

1½ cups grated queso fresco

1½ cups grated white Cheddar cheese

6 large eggs

1 cup milk

Preheat the oven to 350°F, and prepare a gas or charcoal grill for the eggplant, zucchini, and mushrooms.

Slice the chiles lengthwise into 1-inch-wide strips and set aside. Whisk the olive oil and the garlic together in a large bowl, and season with salt and pepper. Toss the eggplant, zucchini, and mushrooms separately in the olive oil mixture just to lightly coat. The eggplant will soak up the most oil, so add more olive oil as needed.

Remove the vegetables from the olive oil and garlic mixture, reserving the remaining oil. Lay the eggplant, zucchini, and mushrooms neatly on the hot grill. Grill the vegetables, flipping once, until they are fairly soft and pliable. The eggplant and mushrooms will take 6 or 7 minutes, and the zucchini 3 or 4 minutes. Remove the vegetables with tongs as they are done.

In a large skillet, heat about 1 tablespoon of the remaining olive oil mixture. Sauté the corn and sweet potatoes over medium heat for about 3 minutes, stirring occasionally so they don't scorch. This will bring out more of the sugar from the vegetables and soften the sweet potatoes so they cook completely in the casserole. Allow to cool slightly.

Grease an 8-inch casserole with some of the remaining oil. When the vegetables have cooled, slice the mushrooms into ¼-inch-thick slices. Lay half the chile strips so they cover most of the bottom of the dish. Layer half of the mushroom slices on top of the chiles, then place a layer of half the corn and sweet potatoes, then place a layer of half the eggplant, then a layer of half the zucchini. Sprinkle with half of each of the cheeses.

Beat the eggs and milk together until well blended. Ladle half the egg mixture over the cheese, shaking the casserole to help the mixture seep all the way to the bottom. Repeat the layering process in the same order, ending with the remaining cheese as the top layer. Pour the rest of the egg mixture over the top, shaking the casserole again to help the mixture seep all the way to the bottom. Bake for 45 minutes to 1 hour, or until the custard is set and the cheese begins to bubble.

Remove from the oven and let the casserole sit for about 15 minutes before serving. This will help all the ingredients firm up, but it will still be quite hot.

Chorizo Chiles Rellenos Casserole

Making a chiles rellenos casserole creates a completely different kind of relleno because the chiles are not stuffed but layered. Instead of dipping the rellenos into the batter, the batter, in this case an egg custard, is cooked with the casserole, setting the ingredients in place. This recipe differs from others rellenos casseroles because I've introduced layers of corn tortillas, which I love for both their flavor and the chewy yet crunchy texture they take on when they are moistened by the cheese, salsa, and custard.

SERVES 6 TO 8

6 large eggs

1 cup milk

8 Anaheim chiles, roasted, peeled, and seeded

1½ pounds Mexican chorizo

2 yellow onions, diced

3½ cups grated Monterey Jack cheese

Coarsely ground fresh black pepper

8 corn tortillas, fried until crisp and broken into 1- to 2-inch pieces (page 27), or 32 corn tortilla chips, broken into 1- to 2-inch pieces

2 cups Salsa Fresca (page 136), coarsely puréed

Preheat the oven to 350°F. Beat the eggs and milk until well blended.

Slice the chiles lengthwise into 1-inch-wide strips. Heat a sauté pan and crumble the chorizo into it, stirring occasionally. When the chorizo begins to release its fat, stir in the onions and cook until the chorizo is cooked through. Stir the mixture occasionally, making sure the chorizo is broken into small, crumbly pieces.

When the chorizo and onions are cooked, drain away any excess grease, reserving a little bit to grease an 8-inch square by 2-inch-high casserole. Lay half of the chile strips on the bottom of the casserole, placing them evenly to cover. Sprinkle half the chorizo evenly over the chiles.

Sprinkle one-third of the cheese evenly over the chorizo. Grate a little fresh black pepper onto the cheese. Ladle half of the egg mixture evenly over the cheese, gently shaking the casserole so the mixture seeps all the way down.

Layer half of the tortilla pieces on the cheese, pressing down so they become fairly flat. Spread half of the puréed salsa fresca over the tortillas. Repeat the entire process, layering first the chiles, then the chorizo, and then the cheese, but this time place the layer of tortilla pieces before you ladle on the remaining egg mixture. Gently shake the casserole again to make sure the mixture seeps all the way down. Spread the remaining half of the salsa on top or the custard, then sprinkle with the last third of the cheese as the final layer.

Bake for 45 minutes to 1 hour, or until the custard is set and the cheese begins to bubble. Remove from the oven, and let the casserole sit for about 15 minutes before serving. This will help all the ingredients firm up, but it will still be quite hot.

Crab Casserole Chiles Rellenos

Be sure to purchase high-quality crab for this recipe. I'm very fond of the Dungeness crab from the West Coast, with its slightly salty-sweet flavor of the sea, but lump crab and Peeky Toe crab are both excellent choices. Steer clear of the artificial crab products or canned crab. Their flavors will not be nearly as enjoyable in this dish.

SERVES 6 TO 8

6 large eggs

1 cup milk

2 tablespoons whole-grain mustard

8 Anaheim chiles, roasted, peeled, and seeded

2 pounds Dungeness or lump crabmeat, picked over to remove all shells

$\frac{1}{2}$ cup finely chopped chives

2 cups seeded and diced tomatoes

Freshly ground black pepper

3 cups grated Monterey Jack cheese

1 cup grated Parmigiano-Reggiano cheese

8 corn tortillas, fried until crisp and broken into 1- to 2-inch pieces (page 27), or 32 corn tortilla chips, broken into 1- to 2-inch pieces

Preheat the oven to 350°F.

Grease an 8-inch square by 2-inch-high casserole with a little butter, oil, or cooking spray.

Whip the eggs, milk, and mustard together until well blended. Slice the chiles lengthwise into 1-inch-wide strips.

Lightly toss the crabmeat, chives, and tomatoes together in a bowl. Lay half of the chile strips on the bottom of the casserole, placing them evenly to cover. Spread one-third of the crab mixture over the chiles.

Ladle one-third of the egg mixture evenly over the cheese, gently shaking the casserole so the mixture seeps all the way through. Layer half of the broken tortillas over the cheese, pressing down so they become fairly flat. Repeat the process with the remaining half of the chiles, the second third of the crab mixture, some more ground pepper, the remainder of the cheeses, the second third of the egg mixture, and the remaining half of the tortillas. Finally, spread the last of the crab mixture on top, followed by the remaining egg mixture.

Bake for 45 minutes to 1 hour, or until the custard is set. Remove from the oven and let the casserole sit for about 15 minutes before serving. This will help all the ingredients firm up, but it will still be quite hot.

Culichi and Shredded Chicken Chiles Rellenos Casserole

Culichi is a rich, somewhat spicy sauce made from poblano chiles, onions, and sour cream. It comes from Culiacán, in the state of Sinaloa on the Pacific Coast. Culichi is often served with fish dishes but I've adapted it here for shredded chicken, where it replaces the traditional egg custard.

SERVES 6 TO 8

8 Anaheim chiles, roasted, seeded, and peeled

2 tablespoons canola oil or other neutral flavored oil

2 yellow onions, finely diced

2 tablespoons chopped garlic

2 bunches green onions, medium-diced

2 tablespoons medium Santa Cruz Chili Powder

2 tablespoons chipotle in adobo, minced with its marinade

2 tomatoes, seeded and medium-diced

4 cups loosely shredded, roasted, or poached chicken meat

1½ cups Monterey Jack cheese, grated

1 teaspoon salt

3 cups Culichi Sauce (page 131)

Preheat oven to 375°F

Slice the chiles lengthwise into 1-inch-wide strips, and set aside. Heat the oil in a large pan and sauté the yellow onions over medium heat, about 5 minutes, until they become quite soft. Add the garlic, and continue cooking about 1 minute so that the garlic releases its flavor. Sprinkle in the chili powder, stir in the chipotle and tomatoes, and simmer for about 2 minutes more. Stir in the chicken meat, season with 1 teaspoon salt, or to taste, and simmer about 3 minutes.

Grease an 8-inch casserole. Layer half of the chile strips to cover as much of as the bottom of the casserole as possible. Spread half the chicken mixture over the chiles. Sprinkle half the cheese over the chicken. Sprinkle half the green onions over the cheese. Ladle half of the Culichi Sauce over the mixture, gently shaking the casserole to help the sauce seep to the bottom of the dish. Layer the remaining chile strips over the cheese and Culichi Sauce. Spread the rest of the chicken mixture over chilies. Sprinkle the remaining cheese over the chicken, followed by the remaining green onions and Culichi Sauce, gently shaking the casserole.

Bake for 45 minutes to 1 hour, until the casserole begins to bubble and brown.

TAKING CONTROL OF YOUR
JALAPEÑOS

While jalapeños are always very spicy, like every chile, they can vary in heat from harvest to harvest with some being hotter than others. Likewise, each of us has a different tolerance for spiciness. I like to use jalapeños for poppers because their size makes them perfect to just pop them in your mouth. If you find that jalapeños are hotter than you like, you can poach them in milk to moderate their heat.

    2 cups milk
    8 jalapeños peeled, seeded,
        and prepared for stuffing

Bring milk to a simmer and poach the jalapeños for about 5 minutes. Remove the pan from the heat and let the jalapeños soak in the milk for about 1 hour. As the chiles cool, the milk will leach some of their heat. Remove the jalapeños from the milk and wipe dry before proceeding.

Shrimp, Ginger, Lemon Grass, and Mint Poppers

I love the Thai flavor combination of ginger, mint, and lemon grass and use it with shrimp in a spicy popper with the beguiling fragrances of Southeast Asia. I make a mousse with half of the shrimp, then fold the remaining shrimp into the mousse.

8 POPPERS

½ pound large (16- to 20-count) shrimp,
    peeled and deveined

½ ounce egg white (white from 1 small egg)

1 tablespoon heavy cream

2 teaspoons canola oil

½ teaspoon freshly chopped garlic

1 teaspoon finely grated ginger

1 teaspoon finely chopped lemon grass

$\frac{1}{2}$ teaspoon finely grated lemon zest

1 teaspoon finely chopped mint

$\frac{1}{2}$ teaspoon minced chives

8 jalapeños, peeled, seeded, and prepared for stuffing (page 19)

Canola or grapeseed oil to fill a large sauté pan $\frac{1}{3}$ inch deep

1 recipe Tempura Batter (page 35)

$\frac{1}{2}$ cup Sweetened Soy for Dipping Sauce (page 138)

Divide the shrimp in half. In a small food processor, purée half the shrimp with the egg white to form a smooth paste. Add the cream in a stream with the motor running. Transfer the shrimp mousse to a bowl and place in the refrigerator. Coarsely chop the remaining shrimp.

Heat the oil in a small sauté pan and gently sauté the garlic for about 1 minute. Add the chopped shrimp, ginger, lemon grass, and lemon zest and continue cooking for 1 to 2 minutes, or until the shrimp begin to turn translucent. Remove from the heat and let the shrimp mixture cool.

When the shrimp has cooled, gently mix in the mint and chives, then fold the shrimp mixture into the shrimp mousse. Using a small spoon, carefully fill each jalapeño.

Heat the canola or grapeseed oil in a large sauté pan. Dip the stuffed jalapeños into the tempura batter, coating them completely except for their stems. Cooking in batches if necessary, place the jalapeños in the oil, leaving enough room to turn them easily without jostling. Cook for about $1\frac{1}{2}$ minutes per side, turning as needed to completely cook the jalapeños. Be careful to control the temperature of the oil so the batter does not scorch. Remove the jalapeños from the pan and place on a rack on top of paper towels to drain off excess oil.

Serve with the dipping sauce.

Smoked Poblano, Mushroom, and Panela Poppers in Blue Cornmeal Crust

I started combining mushrooms and smoked poblano chiles years ago, and I never tire of the smoky, woodsy flavors they make together. With the mild Panela cheese, they are irresistible.

8 POPPERS

5 shiitake mushrooms, stems removed

1 tablespoon olive oil

2 teaspoons coarsely chopped garlic

Pinch of kosher salt

Pinch of freshly ground pepper

2 tablespoons finely diced scallions

3 ounces Panela cheese, at room temperature

3 tablespoons milk

1 smoked poblano chile, peeled, seeded, and diced small

8 jalapeños, peeled, seeded, and prepared for stuffing (page 19)

2 eggs, beaten

2 cups blue cornmeal, for breading

Preheat the oven to 375°F. Prepare a charcoal grill.

Toss the mushrooms in a mixture of the olive oil, garlic, salt, and pepper, and grill over a hot fire for 4 to 5 minutes, turning frequently, until they begin to soften and curl up at the edges.

While they are still hot, coarsely chop the mushrooms, then add the scallions and toss with the mushrooms to wilt them. In a medium or small bowl, blend the Panela and 1 tablespoon of the milk together to create a smooth consistency.

In another bowl, stir the smoked poblanos and grilled mushrooms together.

Work the mushrooms and smoked poblanos into the cheese, combining thoroughly. Using a teaspoon, carefully stuff the jalapeños and seal them shut.

Whisk the remaining 2 tablespoons milk with the eggs and dip the stuffed jalpaeños into the egg wash.

Roll the chiles in the blue cornmeal, coating them completely. Lightly grease a cookie sheet and place the breaded chiles on it. Bake for about 7 minutes, until the cheese melts and the poppers are heated through.

Cabrales, Bacon, and Chive Poppers in Panko Crust

Cabrales, a strong Spanish blue-veined cheese, is delicious with the smoky bacon and the heat from the jalapeño. In this recipe, I fold a little cream cheese into the Cabrales, both to moderate its flavor and to help it melt into a rich, creamy stuffing.

8 POPPERS

2 ounces Cabrales, at room temperature

1 ounce cream cheese, at room temperature

4 ounces bacon, cooked and crumbled

2 teaspoons minced chives

8 jalapeños, peeled, seeded, and prepared for stuffing (page 19)

1 egg

2 tablespoons milk

4 tablespoons flour

4 ounces panko crumbs

Oil for frying

In a small bowl using a fork, blend the Cabrales and cream cheese together. Fold in the bacon and chives.

Put the cheese mixture into a pastry bag with a large, round tip and pipe into the jalapeños, or simply spoon the filling neatly into the chiles, closing the sliced seam shut.

Beat the egg and milk together. Dip the jalapeños in the flour, coat with the egg wash, then roll in the panko crumbs.

Pour the oil into a deep skillet to a depth of $1\frac{1}{2}$ to 2 inches. Heat the oil to 375°F. Immerse the chiles completely in the oil and fry for about 3 minutes, until the breading is golden. Transfer to paper towels to soak up excess oil.

Foie Gras Poppers

Those with a taste for foie gras will love these unusual poppers. Note that the jalapeños are poached and steeped in milk to moderate their heat; otherwise, they would completely overpower the foie gras.

8 POPPERS

2 cups plus 2 tablespoons milk

8 jalapeños, peeled, seeded, and prepared for stuffing (page 19)

8 ounces fresh "A" foie gras, deveined and diced into large pieces

2 ounces Granny Smith apple, peeled and finely diced

1 egg

4 tablespoons flour

4 ounces panko crumbs

½ cup Roasted Corn Vinaigrette (page 135)

Bring 2 cups of the milk to a simmer, and poach the jalapeños for about 5 minutes. Remove the pan from the heat and let the jalapeños soak in the milk for 1 hour to leach some of the heat from the chiles. Remove the jalapeños from the milk and wipe dry.

Sauté the foie gras in a skillet over high heat, stirring constantly, for about 1 minute so that the pieces are still rare in the center but have released quite a bit of their fat. Remove the foie gras, reserving the fat. When the foie gras has cooled, gently fold in the diced apple. Carefully spoon the foie gras mixture into the jalapeños, gently sealing the seam shut.

Beat the egg and remaining 2 tablespoons milk together. Dip the jalapeños in the flour, coat with the egg wash, then roll in the panko crumbs.

Strain the reserved fat from the foie gras through a fine-mesh strainer, and heat it in a skillet over high heat. Carefully place the stuffed jalapeños into the foie gras fat, and cook for about 2 minutes, turning as needed to cook on all sides, until the breading is a bronze golden brown. Serve with the vinaigrette as a dipping sauce.

Seared Sea Scallop, Morel Mushroom, and Fava Bean Salad Rellenos

This salad celebrates spring, when morel mushrooms are foraged, fava beans are in season, sea scallops are sweet and juicy, and fresh tarragon appears in the market. For this dish try to get diver sea scallops which are hand-selected scallops, packed dry, and sold at the market the day they are pulled from the sea, making them the freshest scallops you can buy. An added benefit of diver sea scallops is that the ocean floor is not disrupted when they are harvested, making this method a sustainable harvest technique. I work with foragers in Oregon who hand-harvest mushrooms, and I get very excited when morel season rolls around in late April or early May.

SERVES 6

1 pound sea scallops

4 tablespoons olive oil

½ pound morel mushrooms, cleaned

1 tablespoon butter

1 tablespoon freshly chopped garlic

2 tablespoons brandy

Salt and pepper

1 cup fava beans

¼ pound asparagus tips

2 ounces fresh tarragon

6 tablespoons extra virgin olive oil

2 Meyer lemons

6 poblano chiles, peeled, seeded, and
   prepared for stuffing (page 19)

Remove the connective muscle from the sea scallops and pat them dry. Heat 2 tablespoons of the olive oil in a very hot pan. When the oil is quite hot, and working in batches if necessary, place the scallops in the pan in a single layer, flat side down, allowing a little space between each. Don't move the scallops for about 1½ minutes, or until they begin to turn golden, then flip the scallops and cook for another 1½ minutes. Remove the scallops from the pan and reserve at room temperature if you are going to make the salad right away. Otherwise, refrigerate the cooked scallops until you are ready to use them.

Morels can vary dramatically in size from about ½ inch in length and about ¼ inch in diameter at their widest point to over 3 inches long and about 2½ inches wide. Cut the morels in half or thirds lengthwise or, if they are quite small, leave them whole.

Heat the remaining 2 tablespoons oil in a hot sauté pan and melt the butter in the oil. When the oil and butter begin to sizzle, add the morels and sauté for a couple of minutes, then add the garlic and the brandy, tilting the pan to ignite the brandy with the flame from a gas burner or ignite with a match or lighter. Season with salt and pepper. Lower the heat and continue cooking for another 2 minutes over medium heat. Remove the morels and reserve at room temperature.

To prepare the fava beans, shuck the beans from their shells, then peel the skin from each bean. Blanch the peeled beans in salted boiling water for about 2 minutes, until they turn a bright green and are tender but not mushy. Remove, reserving the water. Shock the blanched beans in ice water, drain, and reserve.

Using the reserved fava-bean water, blanch the asparagus tips for 1 to 2 minutes, depending on their size, until they are tender but still slightly al dente. Then shock in ice water, drain, and reserve.

Slice the scallops into quarters and place them in a bowl with the morels, fava beans, and asparagus tips.

Add the tarragon and toss with the scallops, morels, and fava beans. Toss this mixture with the extra virgin olive oil. Squeeze the lemons over the salad and season with salt and pepper. Divide the salad equally into 6 portions, and stuff into each of the prepared poblano chiles.

Cheddar, Sun-Dried Tomato, and Chorizo Poppers in Tortilla Crust

These spicy poppers are full of the deep, rich flavors of the sun-dried tomatoes, Cheddar, and Mexican chorizo. The crunchy breading of the fried, ground corn tortillas provides great texture and a balancing flavor to the rich filling and spicy chile. Mexican chorizo can be made with ground beef, pork, or a combination of both. It can always be found in Mexican *carnacerias* (meat markets) and is now found in supermarkets as well.

8 POPPERS

3 ounces sharp Cheddar, coarsely grated

1 ounce oil-packed sun-dried tomatoes, finely chopped

4 ounces medium spicy Mexican chorizo, cooked and crumbled

8 jalapeños, peeled, seeded, and prepared for stuffing (page 19)

2 eggs

2 tablespoons milk

4 ounces corn tortillas, fried, cooled, and coarsely ground

Oil for frying

Combine the Cheddar, sun-dried tomatoes, and chorizo, and pack tightly together into cylinder shapes that can slip into the jalapeños. Stuff the jalapeños with the cheese mixture.

Beat the eggs and milk together. Dip the jalapeños in the egg mixture, then into the ground tortillas.

Pour 3 to 4 inches of the oil into a large, heavy skillet and heat to 375°F. Submerge the chiles completely in the oil and fry for about 3 minutes, until the tortillas are golden and the filling is hot.

Queso de Oaxaca, Tomato, and Red Onion Bread Salad Rellenos

Queso de Oaxaca is a creamy, mild cheese that is similar to mozzarella. The use of the partially cooked croutons in the salad provides both texture and flavor.

SERVES 4

3/4 cup extra virgin olive oil

2 tablespoons freshly chopped garlic

1 1/2 cups 3/4-inch cubes French bread or ciabatta

1/2 teaspoon salt

Freshly ground black pepper

2 tablespoons balsamic vinegar

10 ounces queso de Oaxaca, cut into 1/2-inch cubes

1 cup cherry tomatoes, cut in half

1/2 red onion, thinly julienned

3 tablespoons thinly sliced scallions

2 teaspoons seeded and minced jalapeño

3 tablespoons basil, torn into medium-size pieces

4 poblano chiles, peeled, seeded, and prepared
  for stuffing (page 19)

Preheat the oven to 425°F. Combine 6 tablespoons of the olive oil with the garlic in a medium bowl. Toss the bread cubes in the oil and garlic to coat. Season with salt and pepper, and spread the bread cubes on a baking sheet. Place in the oven and cook for about 6 minutes, tossing once or twice, until the bread cubes start to brown on the outside but are still soft in the center. Remove from the oven, let cool, and reserve.

Whisk the remaining 6 tablespoons olive oil and the balsamic vinegar together. In a large bowl, toss the cheese, cherry tomatoes, red onion, scallions, jalapeño, basil, and garlic croutons together. Toss the salad with the olive oil-balsamic vinegar mixture.

Divide the salad into 4 portions, and stuff each portion into one of the poblano chiles, letting the excess salad spill over the sides. Serve at room temperature.

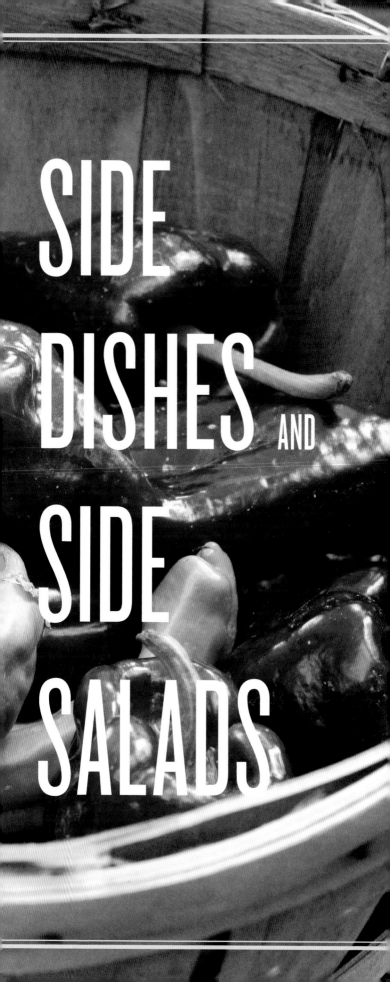

SIDE DISHES AND SIDE SALADS

Black Beans

Black beans are delicious served alongside most rellenos, or they can be refried using the same method as for pinto beans (page 105). Note that in this recipe the beans are salted toward the end of their cooking. This is because they will absorb the salt, which is what you want, but remain soft; however, if you add the salt at the beginning, the beans tend to become tough.

6 CUPS

3 cups dried black beans

3½ quarts water

1 cup medium-diced yellow onion

2 bay leaves

4 tablespoons salt

Freshly ground black pepper

Pick over the beans, rinse, then soak overnight in about 1½ quarts of the water overnight. Drain and rinse the beans.

Combine the beans, onion, and bay leaves in a soup pot, and cover with the remaining 2 quarts water. After the beans have cooked for about 3 hours and are fairly soft, add the salt to the water. (This may sound like a long time, especially after the beans have soaked overnight. Specifying a precise time is tricky as so much depends on factors like the age of the beans and even the altitude. In Colorado, I've cooked previously soaked black beans for as long as 12 hours! If you're closer to sea level, start checking your beans after about 2 hours.)

Continue cooking until the beans are quite soft. Drain and season with pepper.

Refried Beans

Although much of the great flavor of refried beans comes from the lard, rendered bacon fat can also be substituted. If consuming so much saturated fat is a concern, an excellent alternative that will also add flavor is to use oil in which you've made tortilla chips (page 27). Use the oil from the chips, which will have a great flavor, as a substitute for the lard.

To help keep the beans from scorching, choose a very heavy skillet for the refrying. I like to use a large cast-iron skillet because it holds heat well and disperses it evenly.

I QUART

½ cup lard

1 quart Frijoles de la Olla (page 106) with their liquid

¾ cup grated Monterey Jack cheese

Salt and pepper

Heat the lard in a heavy skillet large enough to easily contain all the beans and still allow plenty of space for stirring and smashing the beans. Over medium heat, add the Frijoles de la Olla a little at a time, mashing the beans with a bean or potato masher. As the beans are incorporated into the oil, add more beans. When the beans become too dry to mash, add a little of their cooking liquid to the pan and work it into the mash. Continue this until all the beans have been added and the mash becomes smooth. Lower the heat so the beans don't scorch and stir in the cheese. Season with salt and pepper.

Frijoles de la Olla

This is my simplest recipe for beans and one of my favorites. I serve these beans as a side dish at the restaurant and at home. It translates as "beans of the pot" and refers to the traditional clay pots that beans have been cooked in for centuries in Mexico. Cooking times for beans vary with the age of the beans and the altitude at which they are cooked. The older the beans and the higher the altitude, the longer they will take to cook. Don't salt the beans until near the end of their cooking. You want them to absorb the salt, but if they absorb it at the beginning of the process they will become tough.

2 QUARTS, ABOUT 8 TO 12 SERVINGS

2 cups dried pinto beans

3 tablespoons minced garlic

1 yellow onion, diced

2 Anaheim chiles, peeled, seeded, and diced

1 bay leaf

2 quarts water

1$\frac{1}{2}$ tablespoons salt

1 teaspoon freshly ground black pepper

Pick over and rinse the beans, then soak overnight in water to cover. Drain and rinse the beans and put into a large pot with the garlic, onion, chiles, and bay leaf. Cover with the water and bring to a boil, then reduce the heat and simmer for about 2$\frac{1}{2}$ hours, until the beans are tender but not completely cooked.

Add the salt and pepper to the water, and continue cooking for another 30 minutes or so, until the beans are completely cooked.

Green Rice

I use this spicy rice with several dishes, but it goes particularly well the Calabacitas con Queso Rellenos. In this case, the spice comes from the accompaniment, rather than from the relleno.

I QUART, 4 TO 6 SERVINGS

2 Anaheim chiles, peeled and seeded

1 jalapeño, seeded

1 cup cilantro leaves and stems

4 cloves garlic, peeled

1 tablespoon canola oil

1 cup diced yellow onion

2 cups long-grain white rice

1 tablespoon salt

1 teaspoon black pepper

3½ cups chicken stock

In a blender, purée the chiles, jalapeño, cilantro, and garlic to form a smooth paste.

In a heavy-bottomed saucepan, heat the oil over medium-high heat. Add the onion and sauté for about 2 minutes, until it becomes translucent. Add the rice, salt, and pepper, and stir for about 1 minute. Raise the heat to high, and stir in the chicken stock and puréed chiles.

Cover the rice and, after it comes to a boil, reduce the heat to a simmer, and cook for about 20 minutes, until the liquid is completely absorbed and the rice is cooked through.

Jicama Slaw

Jicama is crunchy and refreshing simply peeled and eaten raw with a little lime juice and chili powder. This recipe was developed to accompany the Lobster and Brie Rellenos with Nantua Sauce.

I CUP

1 cup peeled and very finely diced jicama

1 teaspoon lime juice

2 teaspoons Cilantro Aioli (page 124)

Salt and freshly cracked black pepper

Toss the diced jicama with the lime juice, aioli, and salt and pepper. The creamy aioli helps holds the jicama together, allowing the slaw to be mounded.

Guacamole

Guacamole is only as good as the avocados it is made from. Look for firm yet ripe avocados and cut away any brown spots. I like the Haas avocado because of its high oil content. I also like to leave the avocados chunky, rather than mashing them to make them smooth. Serve the guacamole very soon after preparing it as the avocado tends to brown quickly.

2 CUPS

2 ripe Haas avocados, roughly chopped

1 Roma tomato, seeded and finely diced

1 tablespoon seeded and finely diced jalapeño

2 teaspoons finely chopped garlic

4 tablespoons finely diced red onion

6 tablespoons fresh lime juice

2 tablespoons extra virgin olive oil

Salt and freshly ground black pepper

Gently combine all the ingredients in a large bowl. To keep the guacamole from browning, press plastic wrap directly onto the surface and refrigerate until ready to use.

Mushroom Escabèche

Escabèche are pickled vegetables that are widely used as a garnish with rich food. The acid in the marinade cuts through the richness of the dish, offering a refreshing and contrasting palate cleanser.

ABOUT I QUART

Sachet of 1 tablespoon cumin seeds and
   1 tablespoon fennel seeds

4 cups water

1½ cups cider, white balsamic, or rice wine vinegar

8 cloves

4 sticks cinnamon

3 bay leaves

1 teaspoon salt

2 carrots, roughly chopped

2 red onions, roughly chopped

2 jalapeños, seeded and cut into quarters lengthwise

1 head fennel, coarsely chopped

4 cloves garlic, roughly chopped

1 bunch cilantro

2 pounds button mushrooms

Make a sachet by bundling the cumin and fennel seeds in cheese cloth. Combine the sachet and all the ingredients, except the cilantro and the mushrooms, in a large pot and bring to a simmer for 30 minutes.

Place the mushrooms and cilantro in a noncorrosive bowl and pour the vegetables and liquid over them. Refrigerate. Remove the sachet. Serve cold.

Figs Stuffed with Roasted Walnuts, Queso Casero, and Agave Nectar

Warning: You're going to love these figs so much that you'd be wise to make extra. They are also wonderful served as hors d'oeuvres. The agave nectar is three times sweeter than cane or beet sugar. It is produced in Jalisco from, amongst others, the blue agave which is used in the distillation of tequila. In the case of the nectar, the juice from the core or *piña* of the agave is filtered and heated to turn the carbohydrates into sugar.

4 STUFFED FIGS

4 Mission figs

4 whole walnut halves, roasted

2 tablespoons queso casero

2 teaspoons extra virgin olive oil

2 teaspoons agave nectar

½ ounce rosemary leaves

Preheat the oven to 400°F. Slice each fig into quarters starting from the tip of the stem and stopping just before you reach the end so that the fig remains intact and you can open the quarters with your fingers.

Fill each fig with a walnut and ½ tablespoon of queso casero.

Drizzle with the olive oil and agave nectar and sprinkle with rosemary leaves. Bake for about 6 minutes, until the cheese begins to melt.

Remove from the oven and place each stuffed fig as a garnish for each relleno, then spoon a little bit of the agave nectar and olive oil from the pan over each fig.

Figs Wrapped in Serrano Ham with Whole Roasted Almonds and Roquefort

Figs stuffed and roasted this way are delicious by themselves and make a very special garnish for the Mango, Apple, and Roquefort Rellenos. Serrano ham is a dry ham from Spain, similar to prosciutto. It has a slight gamey flavor and silky fat that lingers on the palate.

4 STUFFED FIGS

4 Mission figs

4 whole blanched almonds, lightly roasted

2 ounces Roquefort

4 thin slices Serrano ham

2 teaspoons extra virgin olive oil

$1/2$ ounce rosemary leaves

Preheat the oven to 325°F. Slice each fig into quarters starting from the tip of the stem and stopping just before the end so that the fig remains intact and you can open the quarters with your fingers.

Fill each fig with a roasted almond and about a quarter of the Roquefort.

Wrap each fig with a slice of Serrano ham and secure with a toothpick. Drizzle the olive oil, sprinkle the rosemary leaves, and bake for about 12 minutes, or until the cheese melts, the figs cook, and the ham begins to get a little crisp.

Bread Salad

A tasty salad on its own, this recipe is also a wonderful complement to the rich flavors of the Goat Cheese and Sun-Dried Tomato Rellenos. I like the little tomatoes because they are packed full of flavor. I make my own blue cornbread, but if that is not an option for you, a darker hearty bread such as pumpernickel is a good alternative.

GARNISH FOR 4 RELLENOS

1 cup canola oil

4 ounces blue cornbread, cut into medium cubes

2 ounces "Sweet 100" tomatoes, cut in half

1 tablespoon finely diced scallion

1 tablespoon coarsely chopped cilantro leaves

Salt and freshly cracked black pepper

4 tablespoons extra virgin olive oil

1½ tablespoons balsamic vinegar

In a small, deep pan, heat the canola oil to 350°F.

Working in batches as necessary, drop in the bread cubes, a few at a time as space permits, and fry for 1 minute or so, until they become crunchy on the outside but are still a bit soft in the center. This way they will absorb some of the vinaigrette without becoming soggy. Drain on paper towels until they cool.

Toss the bread cubes with the tomatoes, scallion, cilantro leaves, and a little salt and black pepper. Whisk the extra virgin olive oil and balsamic vinegar together, and drizzle the vinaigrette onto the bread salad, tossing to evenly coat the ingredients.

Chayote Salad

Once a staple of the Mayan and Aztec diets, chayote squash is now grown in the southern United States and in tropical Latin American climates. It is also found in Cajun and Creole cooking, where it goes by the name *mirliton*. The lime green vegetable is about the size and shape of a pear and has a coarse, somewhat caustic skin that should be removed with a potato peeler. Its seed is large, about the size of an avocado seed. The squash has a fairly neutral flavor, is very crisp, and has a high water content. It can be cooked or eaten raw in a salad.

SERVES 4

1 chayote squash, peeled and seeded

1 green apple, peeled

¼ red onion, thinly sliced in rounds and crisped in ice water

16 orange segments

4 tablespoons extra virgin olive oil

4 tablespoons fresh orange juice

1 ounce pumpkin seeds, toasted, and salted

Using a Japanese mandoline, finely julienne the chayote, followed by the apple. Combine the chayote, apples, onion, and orange segments. Whisk together the olive oil and orange juice, then toss the salad with the vinaigrette; sprinkle with the pumpkin seeds.

Corn Salad

Make this salad at the height of summer, when the local corn is at its sweetest.

SERVES 4

1 to 2 tablespoons olive oil

1 cup corn kernels cut from the cob

1 tablespoon finely diced red bell pepper

1 teaspoon finely diced jalapeño

Kosher salt and freshly ground pepper

2 teaspoons finely diced chives

2 tablespoons Cilantro Aioli (page 124) or regular
   mayonnaise mixed with 1 teaspoon chopped cilantro

Heat a sauté pan with the olive oil and sauté the corn, red pepper, and jalapeño for about 2 minutes. Season with salt and pepper.

Remove from the heat, let cool, and refrigerate. When the salad has cooled, stir in the chives and moisten with just enough aioli to lightly bind the salad.

Orange-Jicama Salad

This very simple salad is a refreshing complement to the Lamb Barbacoa. It's one of my staples, and I sometimes toss it with a little fresh mint and use it to as a garnish.

2 CUPS

1½ cups peeled and coarsely julienned jicama

½ cup finely julienned red onion

½ cup orange segments with their juice

Combine all the ingredients and refrigerate before serving.

Since we opened our first restaurant in the old Hiram Stevens home in back 1983, Tucson has become a thriving community of excellent independent restaurants. Choices range from casual taquerias and sandwich shops to world-class fine dining establishments with a tremendous assortment of ethnic and regional eateries in between. And as Tucson's culinary scene has matured over the years, so have our restaurants.

In 1998 we bid farewell to our downtown adobe home and relocated to the grounds of the Westin La Paloma Resort and Spa in the foothills of the Catalina Mountains. We now have two restaurants, Janos, the highest-rated independent restaurant in Arizona over the last twenty-five years, and J BAR, our casual Latin Grill. I am also the consulting chef for Kai Restaurant at the Sheraton Wild Horse Pass on the Gila Indian Reservation just south of Phoenix. In 2005, we received the coveted AAA Five Diamond award for excellent service and for our unique preparations with native ingredients.

By the time my first cookbook was published in 1989, we had developed about 5,000 recipes. Today, that figure is probably closer to 15,000. Recipe development is one of the most creative parts of a chef's job, and for me the process hasn't changed much. Above all else it requires a good palate, an open mind, and access to great ingredients.

I'm often asked where the inspiration for new recipes comes from. Sometimes, it comes from working with new or unusual products we haven't used before. More often, it's looking at familiar ingredients with fresh eyes or by applying different techniques to them. This can be as simple as learning to make *humitas,* the Central and South American version of Mexican tamales that use fresh corn instead of *masa* or as complex as traveling to Oaxaca to learn how to make authentic barbacoa.

When does a new dish make it on a menu? When its flavors reflect a sense of place and in some way tell a culinary story about where we live. So the next time you find yourself in southern Arizona, give us a call and come by for dinner. We're sure to have something new on the menu and I guarantee that it will contain the authentic flavors of this very special region.

Golden Raisin and Lamb's Lettuce Salad

This is a very light salad to go with the Wild Mushroom and Madeira Rellenos. Lamb's lettuce, also called mâche, has a wonderful texture and flavor that carries the sweetness from the golden raisins and orange zest well. The vinaigrette with walnut oil, orange juice, and white balsamic vinegar is delicious with the salad and plays wonderfully with the woodsy rich relleno.

4 SERVINGS AS A GARNISH

1 tablespoon golden raisins

$1/2$ teaspoon blanched, grated orange zest

1 cup lamb's lettuce

4 small rounds thinly sliced red onion

Kosher salt and freshly ground pepper

2 teaspoons walnut oil

$2/3$ teaspoon orange juice

$2/3$ teaspoon white balsamic vinegar

Gently toss the golden raisins, orange zest, lamb's lettuce, and red onion with the salt and pepper. Whisk the walnut oil, orange juice, and white balsamic vinegar together to create a temporary emulsion. Toss the salad with the vinaigrette.

Verdolagas Salad

Also known as purslane, *verdolagas* grow wild in the washes around southern Arizona and in Mexico. It is prized in this part of the world because its leaves contain an abundance of water captured from the rains. Traditional recipes often call for cooking them with pork and onions. I like to serve this light salad with the Verduras Chiles Rellenos Casserole because its refreshing flavors complement a very rich dish.

SERVES 6

3 cups verdolagas, washed and trimmed of their roots

½ cup tomatoes, seeded and diced small

¼ cup pumpkin seeds, toasted

¼ cup crumbled queso fresco

¼ red onion, julienned

¼ cup pitted and thinly sliced niçoise olives

Salt and pepper to taste

2 tablespoons extra virgin olive oil

1 tablespoon fresh orange juice

Toss the verdolagas, tomatoes, pumpkin seeds, queso fresco, onion, and olives together, and season with salt and pepper. Whisk the olive oil and orange juice together. Toss the salad with the orange juice vinaigrette.

Green Apple–Pecan Salad

This simple little salad was created to accompany the Mango, Apple, and Roquefort Rellenos. It's dressed with a combination of walnut oil and olive oil because by itself the flavor of walnut oil would overwhelm the salad.

SERVES 4

1 Granny Smith apple, peeled

1½ ounces pecans, toasted and coarsely chopped

¼ teaspoon minced chives

2 teaspoons lemon juice

2 teaspoons walnut oil

2 teaspoons extra virgin olive oil

Salt

Using a Japanese mandolin, slice the apple into julienne strips. Toss with the pecans, chives, lemon juice, oils, and salt to taste.

Truffle and Celery Root Salad

I like to serve this salad with the Wild Mushroom and Madeira Rellenos because its herbaceous qualities play wonderfully against the mushrooms, while the truffle reinforces the mushroom flavor in the rellenos. If you want to splurge, slice some fresh truffle over the salad for a real treat.

SERVES 4

2 ounces peeled celery root, julienned

2 ounces fennel bulb, shaved thinly across the bulb with a mandolin

2 teaspoons extra virgin olive oil

Pinch of truffle salt

Several thin slices fresh truffle

Toss the celery root and fennel with the olive oil and truffle salt. Place a small, neat bundle of the salad on each plate, and slice a little fresh truffle over both the salad and the rellenos.

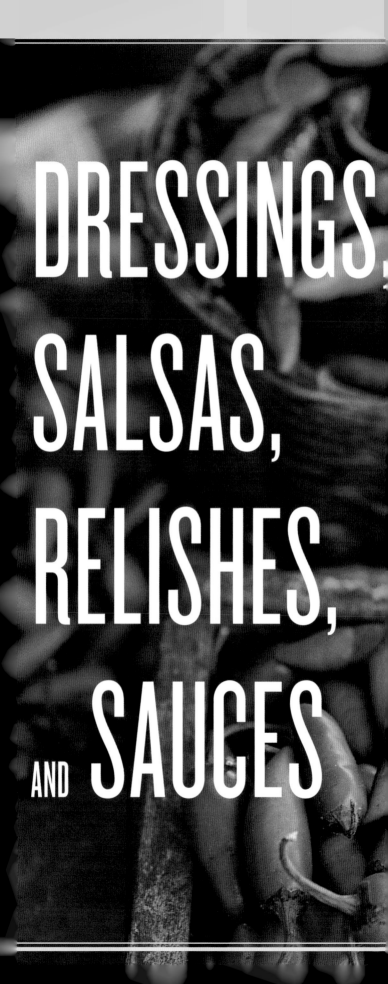

DRESSINGS, SALSAS, RELISHES, AND SAUCES

Cilantro Aioli

This is a basic aioli recipe that can be made in advance and has many other applications in addition to moistening the Corn Salad. I like to spread it on bread for sandwiches or on hot corn on the cob or use it as a dressing for other salads.

2 CUPS

4 egg yolks

1 teaspoon whole-grain mustard

1 teaspoon crushed fresh garlic

$3/4$ cup cilantro leaves with largest stems removed

$1^3/4$ cups light olive or corn oil

5 tablespoons lime juice

Kosher salt and freshly ground black pepper

In a food processor fitted with a stainless steel blade, purée the egg yolks with the mustard, garlic, and cilantro, stopping to scrape down the sides with a spatula as you work. When the cilantro is pretty well chopped, with the motor running, add the olive oil in a slow, steady stream.

When the oil is completely incorporated, the cilantro will be thoroughly puréed.

With the motor still running, add the lime juice in a slow, steady stream until it is completely emulsified. Season with salt and pepper.

Golden Tomato Vinaigrette

I like to make this vinaigrette in the summer when the tomatoes are at their peak. The golden tomato makes a bright, colorful sauce, but red tomatoes will taste just as good. The acid from the vinegar provides a bright, lively edge to the sweet tomatoes.

¾ CUP

2 golden tomatoes, peeled, seeded, and chopped, juice reserved

Pinch of salt

½ teaspoon minced garlic

1 teaspoon minced shallot

6 tablespoons extra virgin olive oil

2 tablespoons champagne vinegar

In a blender, purée the tomato, the salt, the garlic, and the shallot until they are completely smooth. With the motor running, add the olive oil in a slow, steady stream. Once the olive oil is incorporated, with the motor still running, add the champagne vinegar and the reserved tomato juice in a slow, steady stream. Pour into a small glass jar or ceramic bowl and refrigerate. If the vinaigrette separates, reblend.

Cuitlacoche Mojo

This *mojo,* or vinaigrette, has the wonderful flavor of cuitlacoche and a great charcoal-black color. It has many uses besides being served with the Cuitlacoche, Queso Fresco, Corn, Sun-Dried Tomato, and Chipotle Morita Rellenos. I use it to complement many of my dishes at Janos and J BAR when I want something slightly unusual with bright flavor, good acid, and striking color.

2 CUPS

1 cup cuitlacoche

1 jalapeño, seeded

2 tablespoons grated fresh ginger

$1/2$ cup cilantro

4 tablespoons lime juice

2 tablespoons sugar

1 tablespoon kosher salt

$1/2$ cup corn oil

4 tablespoons pineapple juice

In a blender, purée the cuitlacoche, jalapeño, ginger, cilantro, lime juice, sugar, and salt together until smooth. With the motor running, add the oil in a steady stream to emulsify. With the motor still running, add the pineapple juice.

Andalusian Gazpacho Sauce

This recipe is wonderful as a soup, in which case you might prefer to stir all of the vegetable garnishes into it. In this instance, I use the broth for the sauce in the Shrimp, Cabrales, and Chorizo Rellenos, and the vegetables are a layered garnish served alongside the rellenos. This recipe makes about 2 quarts of soup, much more than you'll need to sauce the rellenos. Serve the excess as a first course or side dish with another meal. It's an extremely refreshing gazpacho that goes perfectly with the rellenos.

2 QUARTS

2 thick slices ciabatta or French bread

2 pounds ripest, sweetest tomatoes, chopped

1 tablespoon minced fresh garlic

1 medium cucumber, peeled and seeded

$1/4$ cup extra virgin olive oil

$1/4$ cup Xeres vinegar

$1^1/2$ cups water

Salt and freshly ground pepper

Garnishes:

$1/2$ cup peeled, seeded, and diced red bell pepper

$1/2$ cup peeled, seeded, and diced cucumber

$1/2$ cup diced tomato

$1/4$ cup diced red onion

Place the bread in a small bowl and soak with cold water just to cover, for about 5 to 10 minutes.

Squeeze the bread dry, and place in a food processor with the chopped tomatoes, garlic, cucumber, olive oil, and vinegar and purée. Add up to $1^1/2$ cups water to reach the desired consistency. Strain through a medium-mesh strainer. Garnish as desired.

Caldillo de Tomate

This recipe, courtesy of Zarela Martinez, from *The Food and Life of Oaxaca: Traditional Recipes from Mexico's Heart,* can be varied in many ways by adding chicken stock or various chiles. The sauce is served with many dishes in Oaxaca and is an excellent basic tomato sauce. As always, great fresh tomatoes in season will create the best results. The technique of "frying" the sauce might seem unusual but is common in Oaxacan sauce making. It is akin to the French method of finishing sauces with butter to add sheen and round the flavors.

ABOUT 2½ CUPS

2½ cups very ripe, juicy tomatoes, quartered or cut into large wedges

1 large yellow onion, coarsely chopped

4 cloves garlic, coarsely chopped

½ teaspoon black peppercorns, coarsely crushed

4 whole cloves

3 large sprigs fresh thyme or ½ teaspoon dried thyme, crumbled

2 large sprigs fresh Mediterranean oregano or ½ teaspoon dried Mexican oregano, crumbled

Salt

¼ cup vegetable oil

Place all the ingredients, except for the oil, in a large, heavy noncorrosive saucepan and cook over medium heat, stirring occasionally, until the tomatoes begin to cook in their juices, 5 to 10 minutes. Reduce the heat and simmer, partly covered, stirring occasionally, for another 20 minutes. Let cool. After the sauce has completely cooled, purée in a blender, working in batches if needed, until thoroughly puréed. In a wide, heavy saucepan, heat the vegetable oil over medium-high heat until it begins to ripple. Add the puréed sauce, being careful of the inevitable splattering. Stir vigorously and reduce the heat to low.

Continue cooking, partly covered, stirring occasionally, for about 20 minutes. The sauce can be stored in the refrigerator, tightly covered, for up to three days.

Chiltepín Salsa

The chiltepín is an extremely hot chile. It looks like a small round, red berry about the size of a pea, and although it can be difficult to find, it's well worth the effort to search out. Native Seeds/SEARCH, a nonprofit organization in Tucson, whose mission is to preserve endangered seedlines in Arizona, southern New Mexico, and northern Mexico, sells them online from their website, Nativeseeds.org.

2 CUPS

5 chiltepín chiles

½ chopped white onion

1 tablespoon dried Mexican oregano

4 plum tomatoes, halved and seeded

3 tablespoons distilled white wine vinegar

2 tablespoons tomato paste

Salt

Purée all the ingredients in a blender until completely smooth. Be sure to taste the salsa and season accordingly.

NATIVE SEEDS SEARCH

Native Seeds SEARCH is a non-profit that began in Tucson in 1983, the same year we opened our first restaurant. Its mission is to preserve strains of seeds that are native to Arizona, Southern New Mexico, and Mexico. As ancient native farming practices are replaced by modern methods many indigenous plants have been in danger of extinction. NS/S was created as a seedbank to save the precious native species and to also return them, free of charge to Native American farmers and gardeners in the region. There are now close to 2,500 different seedlines in the seedbank, many of which are available online. Contact them at NativeSeeds.org.

Culichi Sauce

Culichi refers to things that come from the city of Culiacán, which is in the state of Sinaloa on Mexico's Pacific Coast. Culichi sauce is often used with fish, but I include it here for the Culichi and Shredded Chicken Chiles Rellenos Casserole. A very rich sauce, it is also excellent with grilled or pan-fried fish.

3 CUPS

2 teaspoons canola oil or other neutral-flavored oil

1 yellow onion, roughly chopped

3 poblano chiles, peeled, seeded, and roughly chopped

1 tablespoon freshly chopped garlic

2 cups dry white wine

2 cups sour cream

1 cup shredded Monterey Jack cheese

In a 2-quart saucepot with a heavy bottom, heat the oil over medium heat and sauté the onion and poblanos for about 10 minutes, until the onion becomes soft and translucent and the chiles are soft. Add the garlic and continue cooking 1 minute more, so the garlic releases its flavor. Add the white wine and reduce for about 10 minutes to $\frac{1}{2}$ cup. Add the sour cream and bring to a slow simmer, stirring constantly so that the sauce doesn't scorch. Stir in the cheese to melt. Let cool slightly, then purée in a food processor.

Nantua Sauce

This is a classic sauce from the repertoire of French cooking. Its lush creaminess plays wonderfully against the spicy contrast of the chiles rellenos.

2 CUPS

3 tablespoons brandy

3 tablespoons Pernod

1 quart Lobster Stock (page 133)

1 tablespoon tomato paste

1 teaspoon crushed fresh garlic

1 cup heavy cream

Kosher salt

In a small stainless steel saucepot, warm the brandy and Pernod together, and ignite them to cook off the excess alcohol.

Add the lobster stock, tomato paste, and garlic, whisk to combine, and reduce to 1½ cups of liquid over medium heat for about 10 to 15 minutes.

Whisk in the heavy cream and reduce to 2 cups of liquid over medium heat for about 6 minutes. Season with salt, and strain through a fine-mesh strainer.

Lobster Stock

This recipe makes more stock than is called for in any of the sauce recipes. However, stocks are tricky to make in small quantities and too much work not to make in large quantities. Leftover stock can be frozen for later use.

I GALLON

6 pounds lobster bodies

1 pound raw crayfish

³/₄ pound carrots, chopped

³/₄ pound celery, chopped

¹/₃ pound onion, chopped

¹/₃ pound leeks, green and white parts, chopped

¹/₃ pound white mushrooms trimmings (optional)

1 cup brandy

6 tablespoons Pernod

³/₄ cup tomato paste

2 ripe tomatoes, stemmed and roughly chopped

3 cups dry white wine

Sachet of 8 cloves, 12 peppercorns, 1 ounce fresh thyme, and 2 ounces fresh tarragon

Wrap the lobster and crayfish in large resealable bags and pound them with a meat mallet to crush the shells into small pieces and to release the juice from the shells.

In a large stockpot, sauté the carrots, celery, onions, leeks, and mushroom trimmings. Add the lobster and crayfish shells, being sure to include all their juices. Cook the shells, stirring frequently, until they turn bright red, the color of cooked lobster and crayfish.

Pour in the brandy and Pernod, and ignite. When the flames have subsided, mix in the tomato paste, tomato, white wine, and the herb sachet. Add water to cover. Bring to a simmer and cook for 4 to 5 hours, skimming off any foam or impurities that float to the top.

Strain through a coarse strainer or chinois, pushing vigorously on the shells and vegetables to extract all their juice and flavor. Strain again through a fine-mesh chinois.

Champagne Sauce

If you are not familiar with the process of reduction used in French sauce making, you'll be surprised to see that 6 cups of liquid ends up making only 1½ cups of sauce. Flavorful liquids, like the champagne and lobster stock in this case, are cooked down, or reduced, so that excess water evaporates and the flavors of the liquids are intensified.

1½ CUPS

3 cups Brut champagne

3 tablespoons chopped shallots

2 cups Lobster Stock (page 133)

1 cup heavy cream

Combine the champagne and the shallots in a heavy-bottomed saucepan and cook over medium heat for about 15 minutes to reduce the liquid to about ½ cup. Add the lobster stock to the champagne reduction and reduce both, about 7 minutes, to 1 cup of liquid. Add the cream and reduce, about 3 to 4 minutes, to 1½ cups of liquid. Strain through a fine-mesh strainer.

Madeira Sauce

Glace de viande is a super-reduced veal or meat stock. It has huge flavor and a little bit goes a long way. You can make your own by reducing veal stock to a very thick glaze. It is also available at specialty food stores and online.

½ CUP

2 cups Madeira wine

2 tablespoons finely chopped shallots

1 tablespoon finely chopped garlic

2 tablespoons glace de viande

3 tablespoons crème fraîche

Put the Madeira, shallots, and garlic in a saucepan over high heat. Reduce the mixture until there is about ¼ cup left, about 10 minutes. Stir in the glace de viande and the crème fraîche.

Roasted Corn Vinaigrette

We developed this corn vinaigrette to serve with a Yucatan-influenced chicken dish served at J BAR.

2 CUPS

3 ears corn

1½ cups canola oil

1 tablespoon chopped shallots

2 teaspoons chopped fresh garlic

½ cup white balsamic vinegar

Salt and pepper

4 tablespoons lime juice

Preheat the oven to 350°F. Roast the corn in a small amount of the oil until soft but not brown, about 12 minutes.

Let the corn cool, remove the kernels from the cobs, and put the kernels in a blender with the shallots, garlic, and white vinegar and blend until smooth. With the motor running, add the remaining oil in a slow, steady stream to emulsify. Strain. Season with salt and pepper, then whisk in the lime juice. Pour into a squeeze bottle.

Mango Coulis

The tartness of the lime helps bring out the tropical flavors of the mango in this very easy sauce that has many other applications.

¾ CUP

5 ounces ripe, peeled, and seeded mango

2 tablespoons lime juice

Purée the mango and the lime juice together in a food processor or blender. Strain through a fine-mesh strainer.

Salsa Fresca

This is a slightly unorthodox recipe for salsa fresca, but it's my favorite basic salsa. You usually do not find balsamic and red wine vinegars and olive oil in salsa fresca, but I like the balance they provide. The balsamic vinegar adds a deep, round flavor, and the red wine vinegar provides a nice bite. The olive oil brings a little fruitiness and helps to carry the flavors on the palate. This is not a spicy salsa, but it is full of bright, lively flavors.

3 CUPS

2 large tomatoes, chopped

1/2 red onion, finely chopped

3 scallions, finely chopped

1 fresh Anaheim chile, roasted, peeled, seeded, and diced small

1 fresh poblano chile, roasted, peeled, seeded, and diced small

2 tablespoons roughly chopped cilantro leaves

2 teaspoons finely chopped fresh garlic

2 teaspoons balsamic vinegar

2 teaspoons red wine vinegar

1 tablespoon olive oil

Salt and freshly ground pepper

Combine all the ingredients. Refrigerate and serve within 24 hours.

Spicy Pico de Gallo

Pico de gallo literally translated from the Spanish means "rooster's beak." Is the salsa called that because the chiles are reminiscent of the color and shape of the rooster's beak, or because one's tongue may feel like it's been pecked by a rooster's beak after eating the hot salsa, or because the rooster is a metaphor for macho men who eat the spicy condiment with impunity? I've heard all of those reasons, and I'm sure there are others. What we know for certain is that it is a spicy, raw salsa that can be quite hot, as in this recipe. To make it less so, use a milder chile or less of it.

2 CUPS

2 tomatoes, seeded and medium diced

1 white onion, medium diced

2 cloves garlic, finely chopped

2 jalapeños, small diced

1 serrano chile, small diced

3 scallions, chopped

½ cup cilantro, coarsely chopped

2 limes, juiced

Salt and freshly ground pepper

Combine all the ingredients, refrigerate, and serve within 24 hours for optimum flavor.

Sweetened Soy Dipping Sauce

This dipping sauce was created to go with the Shrimp, Ginger, Lemon Grass, and Mint Poppers. Sriracha is Thai hot sauce made from sun-ripened chiles, garlic and vinegar. It is quite hot so a little bit goes a long way. It is now made in the domestically in the U.S. and can be found in most grocery stores.

I CUP

$2/3$ cup dark soy sauce (low sodium works fine for this)

6 tablespoons sugar

2 tablespoons sesame seed oil

4 tablespoons rice wine vinegar

1 teaspoon Sriracha sauce (optional)

In a small saucepan, combine the soy sauce and sugar. Heat, stirring occasionally, until the sugar has completely dissolved. Remove from the heat and whisk in the sesame seed oil and rice wine vinegar. If a hotter sauce is desired, whisk in the Sriracha sauce. This dipping sauce can be stored in an airtight container at room temperature for about a week.

Whisk the sauce together right before serving.

Walnut-Apple Sauce for Holiday Rellenos

Not your typical, thick apple sauce, this is more of a creamy French-style sauce in which the apples and walnuts reinforce the flavors of the relleno. The dried apples have a more concentrated flavor that works well in the sauce.

I CUP

1 teaspoon canola oil

2 tablespoons finely diced yellow onion

3 ounces walnut pieces, toasted

3 ounces dried apples, chopped

1 cup apple juice

1/4 cup cider vinegar

3/4 cup heavy cream

Coat the bottom of a small saucepot with the canola oil and heat over medium heat. Add the onions and sauté just until they soften and become opaque. Add the walnuts and dried apples and sauté together with the onions for 1 minute more.

Add the apple juice and apple cider vinegar, bring to a simmer, and reduce to half the liquid (5 ounces), about 5 minutes over medium heat once it comes to a simmer.

Transfer to a blender and purée until the liquid is quite smooth, then strain through a fine-mesh strainer, being careful to press down on the pulp to extract all the liquid.

Return the purée to the saucepot, whisk in the cream, and reduce by one third (about 1 cup), about 3 minutes over medium heat once it comes to a simmer.

Index